The Simplicity Shift

High-tech products have historically had notoriously poor design. Fortunately, companies have recently started to embrace user-centered design practices. This transition hasn't been smooth, and many companies have trouble transferring good design into final products due to the disconnect between the corporate desire for good design and the corporate culture that implements it.

The Simplicity Shift shows how to shift a company's culture to value, discover and implement simplicity in creating designed products. Companies must move away from the traditional view of product design as a sub-task of a larger sequential process. To create breakthrough, easy-to-use products, companies must elevate design so that its terms and tools are shared by everyone in the team, making design a strategic tool that becomes a part of how everyone in the company thinks, acts, and most importantly, makes decisions.

Scott Jenson is the Vice President of Product Design for Cognima Ltd., London. He has been instrumental in releasing Macintosh and Newton operating systems, developing commercial websites and Symbian mobile phones, and directing dozens of usability trials and focus groups. The holder of several patents and many others pending, he has been doing user interface design and strategic planning for more than 15 years. He was the initial member of the System Software Human Interface group at Apple in the late 1980s, working on System 7 and the Apple Human Interface guidelines. He is a Guest Lecturer at Guildford University. He is also a member of ACM SigCHI and was the past president and founder of the Minneapolis TwinCHI local sigCHI chapter.

The Simplicity Shift

Innovative Design Tactics in a Corporate World

SCOTT JENSON

CAMBRIDGE
UNIVERSITY PRESS

University Printing House, Cambridge CB2 8BS, United Kingdom

One Liberty Plaza, 20th Floor, New York, NY 10006, USA

477 Williamstown Road, Port Melbourne, VIC 3207, Australia

314-321, 3rd Floor, Plot 3, Splendor Forum, Jasola District Centre, New Delhi - 110025, India

79 Anson Road, #06-04/06, Singapore 079906

Cambridge University Press is part of the University of Cambridge.

It furthers the University's mission by disseminating knowledge in the pursuit of education, learning and research at the highest international levels of excellence.

www.cambridge.org
Information on this title: www.cambridge.org/9780521527491

First published 2002

A catalogue record for this publication is available from the British Library

ISBN 978-0-521-52749-1 Paperback

Contents

1 Why Are We Here?

page **1**

THE CHALLENGE 1
THE SOLUTION 2
THE PROBLEM 3
DESIGN IS FREE 4
THE SIMPLICITY SHIFT 5
THE FOUR TYPES OF COMPANY BLINDNESS 6
WHAT THIS BOOK IS NOT ABOUT 7
WHAT THIS BOOK IS ABOUT 8
WHO THIS BOOK IS FOR 8

2 So What Is Simplicity?

11

GOOD INTENTIONS 11
FLEXIBILITY IS THE ROOT OF ALL EVIL 12
EXAMPLE 1: PRODUCT DESIGN AS ADVERTISING 13
EXAMPLE 2: MOBILE PHONE KEYS 14
SIMPLICITY DRIVES UNDERSTANDING 16
SIMPLICITY TAKES COURAGE 16
EXAMPLE 3: BLUETOOTH LOGIN 18
COMMITMENT TO SIMPLICITY 20
CONCLUSION 21

3   You Mean Something Is Wrong?   23

INTRODUCTION   23
CROSSING THE CHASM AND DE-EVOLUTION   24
THE USER INTERFACE DOESN'T EXIST!   27
CONCLUSION   33

4   Design Break: The GPRS Study   35

THE PROBLEM   35
ANALYSIS   36
DISCOVERY 1 – THEY DIDN'T KNOW   37
DISCOVERY 2 – IT WASN'T ALL NEEDED   38
DISCOVERY 3 – DEEP PROBLEMS SURFACED   38
CONCLUSION   39

5   User Blindness   41

INTRODUCTION   41
INSIGHT 1 – PERSONAS: BREAK UP THE MULTIUSER   43
INSIGHT 2 – SCENARIOS: WALK IN THEIR SHOES   50
PUTTING THESE INSIGHTS TOGETHER   54

6   Design Break: Microwave Oven   57

PROBLEM   57
ANALYSIS   60
STAGE 1   64
STAGE 2   66
STAGE 3   68
COSTS   71
WRAP UP   72

7 Feature Blindness 73

INTRODUCTION 73
INSIGHT 3 – UNFEATURES: THERE'S MORE THAN
  MEETS THE EYE 75
INSIGHT 4 – THE PRIORITY TRICK 80
INSIGHT 5 – MAKE THE EASY, EASY AND THE HARD,
  HARD 83
CONCLUSION 89

8 Design Break: MP3 Player 91

PROBLEM 91
ANALYSIS 93
PERSONA AND SCENARIOS 95
STARTING THE DESIGN 102
STAGE 1 103
STAGE 2 105
STAGE 3 106
COSTS 111
SUMMARY 111

9 Innovation Blindness 113

INTRODUCTION 113
INSIGHT 6 – SEE THE WATER 114
INSIGHT 7 – EMBRACE THE IMPOSSIBLE 119
INSIGHT 8 – FAIL FAST 124
CONCLUSION 132

10 Design Break: Heater Timer 133

PROBLEM 133
ANALYSIS 137

STAGE 1 – FIND THE CORE   140
STAGE 2 – EXPAND THE CORE   142
STAGE 3 – BOWING TO REALITY   144
CONCLUSION   148

11 Implementation Blindness   149

INTRODUCTION   149
INSIGHT 9 – THE DESIGN MANIFESTO   152
INSIGHT 10 – THE SWAT TEAM   157
CONCLUSION   160

12 Conclusion   161

WHY WE'RE HERE   161
THE PROBLEM: NAÏVE ATTITUDES   162
USER BLINDNESS   162
FEATURE BLINDNESS   163
INNOVATION BLINDNESS   164
IMPLEMENTATION BLINDNESS   165
THE SOLUTION: ACTIVE INVOLVEMENT   166

Appendix: Recommended Reading   169

Index   171

Why Are We Here?

The trouble with the world is that the stupid are cocksure
and the intelligent are full of doubt.

—*Bertrand Russell*

THE CHALLENGE

Designing innovative consumer products takes both passion and perspective. Passion to overcome the hundreds of problems that always crop up and perspective to know which problems are the most important to solve. Any product that's breaking new ground, almost by karmic definition, must break a few rules. Accepting status-quo design solutions will rarely result in superior products. Breaking new ground in a corporate environment is made even more difficult, however, because projects often have too little time and too little money. Not only must you innovate, but you must do it in half the time. This is the challenge that professional designers must live with every day.

The failure of most consumer products today is in how they meet this challenge. To deliver on extreme time-to-market and cost requirements, consumer products tend to be technology- and feature-driven, cramming in what they can as quickly and cheaply as possible. This inevitably creates cumbersome products – toys that can do much, but are rarely used.

Consumer electronics is becoming a crowded field. No longer is it enough to be there first or to have more features. Products must be simple to understand and use on a daily basis. But, in an industry so often driven by cost reduction and technical novelty, companies are finding that just the desire for a better design isn't enough. Shipping a product requires running a gauntlet of challenges, each of which can compromise a product and make it more complex. *The Simplicity Shift* is about shifting a company culture to value Simplicity in design and to make it the company's most passionate goal. Simplicity is no different than time-to-market, quality, or cost reduction. Simplicity is a deep commitment that must be understood by management, communicated throughout the product process, and rewarded when it's achieved.

THE SOLUTION

The good news is this: the need for quality design is becoming more obvious and the use of "user interface" professionals is steadily increasing. The term User Centered Design (UCD) has started to become commonly used when discussing consumer products. Companies are finally starting to "get it" – design really does matter. Books such as *The Invisible Computer*, by Donald A. Norman (MIT Press, 1999) and *The Inmates are Running the Asylum: Why High Tech Products Drive Us Crazy and How to Restore the Sanity*, by Alan Cooper (Sams, 1999) have found their mark and corporations are rising to the challenge to start building humane products. Much like companies in the 1970s perceived the quality movement, leading companies see an opportunity to differentiate themselves on the basis of usability. The forward-looking companies are starting to make user-centered design a major commitment. If you're not on the bandwagon, then you're behind your competition.

A growing maturity also exists in the UCD community about how to achieve this. Instead of following the classic technology-led process, which is the base of most companies today, turn the whole process around. Replace the technology process with one based on understanding who the users are and what their needs are. Once this is understood, sculpt the product design around this understanding, bending technology to fit these well-grounded needs.

THE PROBLEM

Never has an approach been so intuitively correct. And never has an approach been so abysmally executed. Even when companies that "get it" do the user studies, upfront designs, and prototypes, much of it ends up on the floor, and the actual product becomes a pale shadow of the original design. My experience, both within companies as the director of the design department, and as a consultant, has shown me that companies can kill good design ideas in a hundred different ways. The most common cause is simple naiveté: the company doesn't understand the deep management commitment required to take an innovative new design and see it all the way through to final delivery.

Even more striking are the companies that hire the design consultant or have an internal design department and refuse to choose a new design because it appears too costly. This perceived cost usually comes in three forms. The first is the view that a simpler product has a high-opportunity cost. A new, simpler design is often seen as too radical, making too many assumptions about what the consumer needs. Fear exists that the power of the product is somehow diminished. Simple designs have a tendency to make product managers nervous because they view the design as not having enough features to be competitive. This is a bit odd to a designer. It seems to mean if a product doesn't look complex enough, it can't be used by real customers. This is a complete fallacy because designs can be simple, yet hide power features beneath the surface. Everyone can win.

The second perceived cost is that the design isn't practical to implement. For example, the design could automate a previously complex sequence of tasks, but this automation might require some tricky programming. These types of design jumps, which require initially unknown amounts of programming work, don't fit within the previous obvious ways of doing things. At first blush, the design appears to be far too ambitious. This is also a fallacy because, while designs might have grand plans, a technical path nearly always exists that can achieve the essence of the design goal without too much pain.

The third, and final, perceived cost comes from the apparent expense of using UCD in a product. This often comes from bad initial positioning; UCD hasn't been considered a first-class citizen. UCD is usually added near the end of a project when it's too late to change most things and design at this stage of a project usually finds more problems than it can fix. When executed in this way, design appears to cause delays and incur cost. Design is seen as expensive because it's set up to fail. It's done too late to have a positive impact on the product.

These perceived costs keep many companies from considering designs that could lead to innovative products and even cause some teams to actively avoid using interaction designers. To be fair, many innovative designs require some additional work and might not be practical or make business sense. To achieve simple design, you must be able to discuss the issues deeply and make informed business tradeoffs. Companies do this all the time, of course, balancing difficult issues, such as time to market, quality, and cost. These traditional issues are critical to the company, often requiring difficult decisions and forcing strategic changes.

Design is no different. It affects business strategy just as forcefully as these traditional issues. Design must have equal weight and be valued by the entire product team from the beginning of the project.

DESIGN IS FREE

This situation with design today is similar to the role of quality in the 1960s when Philip Crosby wrote "Quality Is Free." At that time, numerous misconceptions existed about what quality was and how it was achieved. Quality was valued and attempts were made to improve the commitment of a company to quality. More often than not, however, new improvements were just as quickly lost. Quality simply wouldn't stick to a corporate culture.

Crosby's diagnosis was this: a company needed to pass through a clear management maturity scale to make quality, properly and permanently, an integral part of the company culture. Just wanting quality wasn't enough and establishing a quality department wasn't enough. A deep cultural and managerial shift had to exist that reflected the commitment to quality. You couldn't treat quality as if it were a fad – something to be tacked on to the end of a project.

The same situation occurs today with Simplicity in design. Good, radically simple product design has value and most companies want this type of product. Just as with quality in the '60s, however, you don't get it through quick fixes. Companies need to mature their approach to design much like they did with quality. You don't get design by simply creating a design department. While this is a nice start, it only puts an artificial box around the problem. The real work comes when you discuss how the design department informs the strategic planning of the company, how it helps the project management process, and how it works with the development team. Once design becomes an integral part of a company's development process, design – like quality – can become free.

THE SIMPLICITY SHIFT

The world is on the brink of taking UCD seriously. Companies have been inspired by the good examples and they're making a sincere effort to learn from them. Unfortunately, the path to complexity is paved with good intensions. Although many companies want a good, simple product, they end up getting much less. This isn't intentional. This is through a lack of maturity. Simple ideas are fragile ideas and a thousand things can turn them into a design disaster. Marketing has just decided to add three new requirements to the product. Development can't implement pop-up menus. Can't you use icons instead? The product cost is too high, so we'll have to reduce the screen size by half. Can you rework the screen shots by next week? Complexity is what fills the gaps in poor execution.

The Simplicity Shift is about closing the gap between the willing spirit and the weak body. Good design doesn't simply happen as an afterthought. You must make it your most passionate goal. You have to set up a managerial process that values design, resolves the issues it raises, and then has the guts to carry the design through. You do this by making a shift in your company – a Simplicity Shift.

Simplicity goes beyond a term like "good user interface," which has become so broad, it has little clear meaning. Simplicity is a goal with precision. *Simplicity* means streamlining, pruning clutter, cleaning up presentation, and improving the initial experience with a product. But Simplicity is more than just making a cute product for technophobes. Simplicity streamlines and optimizes use, as well. Power users don't want to follow a complex sequence of steps any more than the novice user: Simplicity has value for everyone.

The Shift comes in the culture surrounding a product. A company doesn't get a simple product only by hiring good user-interface designers. While that's a nice start, a designer's best efforts have a difficult path to final release. To conquer the previously described complexity, a company must appreciate the difficulties involved in designing, and then shipping a simple, breakthrough product. The Simplicity Shift is about the tools necessary to shift a company's culture to accomplish this.

THE FOUR TYPES OF COMPANY BLINDNESS

Companies today have little insight into what Simplicity is in a consumer product and how it can be achieved. In my experience, most companies today have four stages of blindness that prevent them from seeing what they should be doing: user blindness, feature blindness, innovation blindness, and implementation blindness. These types of blindness are the root misconceptions and bad practices that set up product teams to fail before they even start.

User blindness comes from thinking you know who the user is. Some people implicitly assume the user is someone just like themselves, others – often marketing managers – assume it's a conglomeration of all users, a multiuser who requires everything under the sun. Both approaches prevent you from seeing the true user and understanding what that user needs from your product.

Feature blindness comes from being awash in sophisticated features. Usually, so many must be crammed into the product, the design becomes muddled and hard to understand. While the sheer number of features is a large part of the problem, the real cause of the trouble is the implied need to show them all at once. By creating a cornucopia of features, the product ends up overwhelming the users, so they don't know where to start with the product.

Innovation blindness comes in two forms. The first is the team not realizing they're surrounded by design defaults that restrict their thinking and prevent consideration of new ideas. Once these new ideas make it on the table, however, they aren't considered because they're seen as too hard to achieve. Innovative ideas happen surprisingly often. They're simply killed off much too quickly.

Implementation blindness comes from not understanding that a complete design is only the first major milestone. Getting the product shipped is where the real work begins. Many companies don't see that a product design can lose its path a thousand times over when moving from design to shipping. The design that usually makes it out the door rarely matches the vitality of the original concept.

Once a company has been cured of these types of blindness, a new product culture can arise. A culture that can discuss and discover Simplicity, make difficult decisions as to what should go in or out of the product, execute those decisions, and, finally, bring them to market.

WHAT THIS BOOK IS NOT ABOUT

This isn't a book about design tips and tricks. I won't tell you how to use white space effectively or about clever ways to use fonts and color to increase information density. I also won't cover techniques to improve your user-testing reports or new discoveries in field research. These topics have already been covered in many good books. An appendix at the back of the book refers you to books that cover these topics in more detail.

WHAT THIS BOOK IS ABOUT

This book is about design insight and management. It focuses on the design tools that companies must share across their senior management, project managers and team members, to ensure that everyone works together to make the project successful.

The initial two chapters layout a few terms and concepts that need to be established before we can begin. The remainder of the book is organized around the types of design blindness, explaining each and giving examples. Each blindness will have insights that are specific actions you can take to improve your company's ability to understand problems, discuss them, and make decisions that create Simplicity in your products. Intermixed between these chapters are Design Breaks which show how these insights can be used in real world situations.

WHO THIS BOOK IS FOR

Most experienced designers will be well versed in the insights I reference in this book. Knowing the tools isn't all that counts, though. Using the tools with the right people at the right time makes all the difference.

I hope this book has value to both designers and managers. How to do design is becoming well understood. How to manage design still has a long way to go. I find designing consumer products an exciting and rewarding activity because the potential is great. You can design products that will make a difference.

I also hope this book will be useful to small companies without much of an established design culture. Big companies tend to have design expertise. Their problems lie in learning how to unlock the power of these internal groups. Small companies have little to start with and feel that good design is only for the big boys. Small companies must realize that most bad design comes not from a lack of design experience, but from a series of bad management decisions. Bad products are usually set up to fail from the beginning. If you can get the management on board, you can make amazing products.

I truly feel design can be free. While throwing money at any problem can certainly help, most of the techniques described in this book can be done with moderate cost and still make a large impact on a product's Simplicity. I hope this book can encourage companies to start to Think Simple and create that internal creative spark that enables them to make breakthrough products.

So What Is Simplicity?

Simplicity is the peak of civilization.

—*Jessie Sampter*

GOOD INTENTIONS

Complexity is the most common problem in bad product design. Complexity isn't introduced on purpose, of course, it simply seeps in. When products lack clear design direction, complexity is what happens by default. It shows up slowly, adding an icon here, asking the user another question there. These additions are always well intentioned because they're trying to solve a valid problem, but as I noted in the previous chapter, the road to complexity hell is always paved with good intentions.

Simplicity is the antidote and what product design must be about. Simplicity comes from a basic observation: all products are used in much the same way the vast majority of the time. This is true for expert users as much as for novices. Take any consumer product, such as a mobile phone, a digital camera, or an MP3 player. Even the most complex versions of these products have to dial a number, zoom the lens, or pause the playback. If these core tasks are cumbersome or complex, you affect every user, even the expert.

Unfortunately, fancy new features are all too commonly added to a successful product, and these core features get compromised and made more difficult to use. Offering everything to the user at once simply isn't possible. By cramming more features into a product, something has to give and, often, the Simplicity of the core features gets lost in the shuffle. Simplicity is about lowering the priority of the high-end functionality to make sure the core tasks work exceedingly well.

Having been in the high-tech industry for many years now, I can safely say that 99 percent of most product discussion takes place around functionality. For example, I often hear comments like "our new product requires features X, Y, and Z" or "we have an existing product that must be made competitive by adding feature Q." Meetings and strategy sessions usually focus on *adding* features. Rarely does any discussion occur about simplifying the product or changing the feature mix that already exists.

This doesn't mean Simplicity isn't asked for repeatedly in product meetings. A product manager who doesn't want a "simpler, more user-friendly" product is hard to find. The problem lies with a poor understanding of what these words mean and, more importantly, the real commitment and hard work they will take to achieve it. Unfortunately, when some managers ask for a simple user interface, what they're asking is "give me every feature possible and fix the interface up as best you can, so it doesn't look completely ridiculous."

FLEXIBILITY IS THE ROOT OF ALL EVIL

The majority of the time, complexity can be traced to a single design approach: offering too much flexibility. Notice I didn't say flexibility itself is evil – products do need to bend and mold to the user. My point is too much flexibility is the root cause of most design problems.

High-tech products with embedded microprocessors are capable of adding large amounts of functionality to a product fairly inexpensively. Most product managers believe it's a waste not to offer this to the user. The problem with this large offering is it tends to bury the product in options, which require significant numbers of decisions from the user just to do something fairly simple.

What usually happens to most consumers when faced with a button-studded remote control or a long list of icons is a type of paralysis I call *parsing shock.* Consumers are stunned by the number of choices, spending much of their energy trying to understand this vast array of options, so they can formulate a problem-solving strategy. They don't know where to start. In effect, consumers don't know what to ignore.

1 + 1 = 3

Edward Tufte wrote about information design and he had a simple graphic rule: $1 + 1 = 3$. The idea is that when you draw a single line, you have only that line. Drawing a second parallel line, however, adds two new items to the graphic – the second line and the white space in between. A strong correlation exists to this rule in product design. Having two features on display is more than twice as complex as having only one feature. In addition to the buttons, a third task is created: the choice of knowing which of these two buttons to pick.

Simplicity comes from being ruthless in what you initially show the users, so you can reduce their parsing shock when trying to accomplish the core tasks. This reduction usually isn't difficult. Having the perspective to make this decision and the courage to see it through, however, is the real challenge. This book offers tools to make this easier.

EXAMPLE 1: PRODUCT DESIGN AS ADVERTISING

I was working on a messaging application for a mobile phone a few years ago and saw how complexity can creep into a product. The device had a small keyboard and a large screen with no touch-screen input. For most screen interaction, the device relied on four hardware buttons down the right side of the display with "soft labels" next to them on the screen. In addition, a menu button brought up a standard onscreen menu for more choices.

My team had already put together a simple messaging design. They had done their homework and identified the two high-priority tasks as the reading and deleting of new messages. To make these two tasks simple and easy to use, the team used two of the soft buttons on the right. A third button, New, brought up a choice of message types (SMS, E-mail, Fax) in a small pop up.

The marketing department of our partner company was adamant that the top-level view of the messaging application show off the deep power of the device and insisted the top-level buttons be Open, New E-mail, New SMS, and New Fax. This caused Delete to get kicked out the window.

To get Delete back in, a completely separate folder view had to be created, which you needed to switch into, before you could delete any messages. This, of course, was one of our highest priority tasks and it was now buried into a separate view that you had to navigate to through the Menu button. The user, who would rarely send faxes or e-mails, now had to dig through the menu structure to discover how to delete a message. Not only that – now an additional view existed for the user to understand and cope with.

This is a classic example of design being massively impacted by business marketing needs. I sympathize with marketing's desire to ensure the value of the device was readily apparent to the user, but an enormous cost arose from this decision. The device is now much more difficult to use, and even more so for advanced users because they get more mail traffic than novices.

EXAMPLE 2: MOBILE PHONE KEYS

One of the clearest examples of a company's continual commitment to Simplicity comes from mobile phones. It's widely accepted that Nokia's stunning market share growth from 1996 to 2001 was based in large part on the Simplicity of its interaction design. Clearly, other factors, such as interchangeable face plates and fashionable industrial design, also had a strong impact. However, few people in the industry would dispute that the Nokia screen design was far better than most.

Nokia rapidly evolved its phone throughout the 1990s. Starting off with the fairly cumbersome 2100 series, which had eight main keys

2100
8 buttons

6100
6 buttons

5100
4 buttons

FIGURE 2-1. Nokia's constant push for Simplicity in handset design.

above the numeric keypad. Nokia improved on this significantly with the 6100 series, which had only six buttons: up, down, dial, hang up, left soft key, and right soft key.

The 6100 series was seen as one of the best designs in the industry. But, with the new 5100 series, Nokia went even further and reduced this down to only four buttons: up, down, select, and back. (See Fig. 2-1.)

The motivation of this Simplicity was the understanding that only two tasks were used the majority of the time: answering the phone and dialing from the phone book. Nokia came up with an extremely simple and elegant design to do this. Answer the phone? Press the big button. Hang up the phone? Press the big button. Call someone? Use the arrow keys to get to the right person and press the big button. By restricting the number of buttons and using them cleverly, the phone had an un-cluttered look. As my teenage son said one day when we were discussing various phones, "Anyone can use a Nokia."

SIMPLICITY DRIVES UNDERSTANDING

This example shows how Simplicity, in this case through choice re-duction, enhances the learning process and streamlines the use of the product. The big button answers the phone and hangs up. The up/down arrows take you directly to your phone book entries. There aren't many options because there aren't many buttons. Users can quickly discover the fairly simple functional choices.

I occasionally hear from power users that designing a simple product is an insult to the expert. Simplicity, however, doesn't have to mean impoverished. It simply means prioritized. By having the simple tasks clean and obvious, you improve not only the learning of the product, but also the ease of use. With the Nokia example, the four-button design creates a type of *scaffolding*, which enables you to use the phone in a basic manner immediately. This not only drives comfort and confidence in the phone for novices, but also provides a quick and efficient path for advanced users. Once you grow beyond this basic path, the Menu area exists for those who want to explore and use all the cool advanced features. Simplicity is a win/win scenario.

SIMPLICITY TAKES COURAGE

Appreciating the guts it took for Nokia to bring this new design to market is difficult. The company already had an existing design in the 6100 series, which was generally perceived as working well and a significant improvement to the original eight-button design. But Nokia understood the consumer benefit of Simplicity and that reduc-ing the button count would affect the perceived complexity of the device. This doesn't all come free, however. Some tasks with the four-button design are harder to do than with the original six-button design. Editing a contact, for example, has a few more steps than in the original.

Nokia clearly decided to make a few secondary functions harder, which seems counterproductive. But editing a contact wasn't the core use for the product; it was answering and dialing. Doing this with four buttons instead of six was taking advantage of the $1 + 1 = 3$ principle in reverse. Doing the same thing with 50 percent fewer buttons feels significantly more obvious and easier. The new design was clearly a win and made huge inroads for Nokia into the low-end phone space. Making this type of easy/hard tradeoff is at the core of capturing Simplicity. It's a tradeoff that's difficult for many to make because making a task slightly harder to access is completely contrary to our natural "make everything easy" instincts.

Simply reducing buttons isn't the goal, however. Many bad products out there, such as digital watches, have few buttons and are, of course, excruciating to use. The goal is to meet the core user's needs through a simple design, which is easy to use. If this can be done with fewer buttons, the perceived Simplicity of the device will be greatly enhanced.

Shipping a simple design is much harder than it looks. Always pushing and trying to simplify the product takes courage: saying this is just good enough is easy. Nokia didn't stop with the six-button design, which was good. The company continued to push and came out with a four-button design shortly thereafter. Making some tasks slightly harder to keep the core tasks streamlined also takes courage. This book calls out tools that will help you make these types of decisions, although this isn't a mathematical process. You can do all the exercises and get a much stronger idea of which way to go but, sometimes, you must make a judgment call. This is where courage comes into play. You have to see and appreciate examples of Simplicity to appreciate this tradeoff. Tools can help a great deal, but you have to use your gut at some point. The more you see and appreciate those good examples around you, such as the Nokia keypad example, the better able you'll be to make that jump.

EXAMPLE 3: BLUETOOTH LOGIN

In another project, there was a big push to use Bluetooth in our next generation of mobile phones. *Bluetooth* is a radio technology that enables you to share audio and data traffic over a short distance. Bluetooth is another one of those cool new technologies that everyone was getting excited about. Instead of messy, slow wires, you can now have your phone in your briefcase while you use a tiny wireless headset. Very cool indeed.

The high-level benefits of a technology are easy to get excited about, but getting it to work without numerous complex steps is yet another challenge. Let's walk through what the users had to do to use something as simple as a headset with their new phones.

1. Take your new phone and new headset out of the box and turn them on.

2. Navigate to and open the Bluetooth control panel on the phone.

3. Search for Headsets.

4. Select your headset (only one will be in the display).

5. Choose Pair.

6. Type in your headset pass code.

7. Close the Bluetooth control panel.

8. Open the Profiles control panel.

9. Switch to Bluetooth headset.

10. Close the Profiles control panel.

Quite a gauntlet of tasks to get through. I find this striking because Bluetooth is a technology meant to be used by millions. Imagining that many consumers could have a challenging time setting this up isn't difficult. Now, if users were meant to be pairing with up to a dozen devices, I can see how such a highly functional control panel would be of some use. Initially, though, the vast majority of use for this technology was to hook up a phone to a headset — a simple task that appears overwhelmed by this long sequence of steps.

The feature, using radio to eliminate wires, seems a good thing, but the execution left much to be desired. My design team's response was to list what the user needed to have happen and to create a goal from the team's point of view. Suspend disbelief for a moment and pretend everything is magic. What would be the best solution for the user? This seems straightforward:

Open the box, take them out, and turn them on. They work together!

The problem, of course, is that there are many technical reasons why this is difficult to achieve. But this is one of the key starting points for Simplicity. It isn't technically obvious how to achieve it at first. What motivates you is it's the right thing to do. You have to suspend technical disbelief long enough to see the user value, and then try and be clever enough to figure out a practical solution to the problem.

I know immediately why my magic solution will face strong opposition. The Bluetooth technical specification doesn't even begin to talk about how this type of automatic paring could take place. Instead, it talks about the maximum number of paired devices and doesn't make the rather obvious admission that, at least initially, only one probably exists! All the specification offers is the raw flexibility to allow anything to be added at any time. Of course, this flexibility makes the most important item you want to add to your phone nearly overwhelming. Flexibility is the root of all evil.

But, if a product team valued and pursued Simplicity, a fun and cooperative brainstorming session would evolve a solution that might get close to the magic ideal. For example, assume that complex control panel solution remains in the product. This keeps the high-end case of attaching anything to the phone in place and not compromised. I'm not too worried because, at least for now, this will almost never happen. This reduces the problem to a much simpler one: How do I attach a headset to my phone?

For example, what if when the power is on, the phone does a quick peek for headsets, if it doesn't already have one configured? If the phone does find headsets, it pairs with them, using the default pass code, 0000, which will work for 99 percent of all headsets. Voilá, you have your magic solution!

I've been in these meetings enough times that even this modified proposal will provoke strong reaction from the technologists. They'll most likely dissent, saying that looking for a Bluetooth headset each time you turn on the device will waste the battery, slow boot time, etc., etc., etc. Fine. Discuss these tradeoffs and ask how bad they are. And, if they are all that bad, ask what can be done to reduce these problems, and so forth. Most programmers' concerns are, indeed, valid. I've also found that getting programmers involved with the challenge almost always gets their formidable puzzle-solving abilities involved and a fairly good compromise solution is usually found.

Simplicity begins in trying to see a grander vision that isn't filtered by technology. You'll never find Simplicity if you don't try to look beyond the obvious issues in front of you. Once you do find something, the next step is not to roll over and give up when you find out a beautifully simple solution is difficult or even impossible. What you have to do is find a practical way to achieve most of this goal.

COMMITMENT TO SIMPLICITY

This example leads me into the broader point of having a commitment to Simplicity. This might seem a bit obvious, but companies will never get Simplicity without actively pursuing it. Unfortunately, most companies don't. They don't have the tools to uncover a simpler design or the insight to make the tough decisions to make the simpler design happen.

When I explain this to project managers, they get nervous. Of course, they want Simplicity, but they quickly add, not *too* simple. They are concerned I'll tip the scale too far and create a product that's too boring or even uncompetitive. This is a frustrating, but understandable, response. First, you must understand that Simplicity is a feature! Simplicity is a key differentiation in a product. Second, Simplicity isn't about removing features – it's about prioritizing them. Find the core and make it wonderful. Then gently layer on the additional features, but make sure they don't compromise the core design.

When Crosby wrote "Quality Is Free," he created a maturity scale to grade companies as to how well quality was seen and used. The higher up the maturity scale a company was located, the more likely the quality program would be effective. Design is no different.

I'll use a similar system to Crosby's. Level 1, the lowest level of the maturity scale is ignorance, which is not knowing what Simplicity or good design is. In Level 2, the company knows about and wants better-designed products, but isn't making the commitment to make this happen. With Level 3, a dedicated effort exists where Simplicity is sold, incorporated, and valued throughout the company. Level 4 is a Zenlike perfection where good design is expected at every level. The processes are so well ingrained that when a problem occurs with the design of a product, explaining why the design was less than perfect is possible.

Because you're reading this book, you're at least at Level 2. Unfortunately, companies have difficulty rising above Level 2 because most of the team needs to be at the same level for it to work. Many examples exist of design departments operating at a much higher maturity level than the rest of their company, yet the overall attitude of the company keeps it at Level 2 or less.

Often the biggest concern about introducing a design-improvement effort is it will delay a project, and add cost and hassle. What I find particularly poetic is that often, a simpler design reduces the amount of work and cost in a product, making it less expensive and faster to market. This is one reason why I say design is free.

Getting too carried away with the levels, and how you go from one to the other, is a bit of a tedious exercise. The important point is that you don't get Simplicity by hiring one designer and sticking him or her in the back room. Breakthrough Simplicity comes from an actively valued cultural commitment, measured and managed by top company management.

CONCLUSION

Simplicity, once you see it, becomes infectious. You can see the power it has to sweep away the flotsam and jetsam of creeping complexity.

But, the most serious challenge to getting Simplicity into a product is political. It takes courage to create a simple product because some will think it's too simple. Power users who won't do exactly what they want have a loud voice indeed. For many product managers, ignoring a cry for a feature is like ignoring the cry of a hungry baby. If you're able to do it, it still feels horribly wrong.

The remainder of this book covers the tools to calm these fears and prioritizes your thinking so you don't design by the path of least resistance but, instead, you can design by insight. You will make difficult decisions, but they'll be the decisions that create a breakthrough design, which still meet the needs of all your users.

You Mean Something Is Wrong?

3

> *The greatest obstacle to discovery is not ignorance – it is the illusion of knowledge.*
>
> —*Daniel Boorstin*

INTRODUCTION

Simplicity is a goal that few try to obtain. Part of the problem is some companies don't really see that anything is really wrong with the product process. There are two central concepts I see misunderstood and misused within companies that must be called out and corrected if we are to make progress on executing Simplicity.

The first concept I want to correct is a marketing model proposed by Geoffrey A. Moore in his book, *Crossing the Chasm: Marketing and Selling High-Tech Products to Mainstream Customers* (Harperbusiness, 1999). Nothing is wrong with his model. I don't want to call that into question. The problem I see is how his model is utilized. His marketing model is misused when applied to new product development.

The second concept I need to correct is a confusing and dangerous use of the term "User Interface." I make the claim that, in product development, the user interface exists only as a project-planning fiction; a bad fiction used by old-guard product managers. What the user interface is and how it affects not only a product, but also the company itself, is much more complex than most people appreciate.

CROSSING THE CHASM AND DE-EVOLUTION

Tent Evolution: Slow, Continual Evolution

Let's take an example from another, different business domain: camping tents. When I was 18 years old, I bought a lightweight tent for my grand adventure of bicycling across Europe. I bought another, similar, tent for my sons to use 20 years later. The tent industry probably doesn't follow a user-centered design process, but the improvements in my tent are exactly the types of improvements you see in the software industry. The new tent did more, cost less, was more convenient, and even had nice touches, such as better zipper pulls and pocket placements. The new tent was a better tent in every way. In addition, the new tent was one-half the cost! Did a huge design consultancy that specialized in user-centered design create this product? Not at all. All that happened was 20 years passed, with dozens of companies iterating hundreds of different tent designs. The good companies listened to their customers, used their own products, and generally matured and evolved better designs slowly. This took awhile, but I ended up with a vastly improved tent.

Tent evolution is an example of the gradual steady improvement of a stable product concept. If we had warped my new tent back in time 20 years to my earlier self, my younger counterpart would have been able to pitch and use both tents. The concept hadn't changed significantly. A better tent, for the most part, is a universal concept.

Crossing the Chasm

The same stable nature doesn't hold with high tech consumer products. Moore proposes a "technology adoption life cycle," which describes how new disruptive technologies are accepted by the consumer public. He divides consumers into five user groups. At the front end of the scale are *innovators* and *early adopters*, who quickly embrace technology and its costs. Bringing up the rear are laggards, who are more concerned with convenience, cost, reliability, and ease of use. Good examples of early adopters are those brave souls who carried Apple IIs with VisiCalc through the back doors of their companies. They weren't highly trained engineers, but they were actually a surprisingly broad range of people who had the foresight to see the value of this new tool. Most importantly, they persevered when it was a challenging tool to use. The high-tech industry exploded by taking these early adopters on board as their primary customers.

Innovators and early adopters are a considerably small portion of the consumer population. The remainder of the consumer spectrum's level of patience tails offs quickly. The further down the line, the less patience is exhibited toward high-tech products. These laggards tend to wait on the sidelines, not purchasing a new product until the perceived cost of using the product goes down. This is the chasm Moore is concerned about. As the high-tech industry tends to create products for the early adopters, how is it possible to present and sell these products further down this consumer spectrum? Moore's book is really about marketing. It optimistically assumes the products are relevant and well designed, but that the change in behavior required for the adoption of these new products is a significant marketing hurdle. Moore's model of the consumer spectrum and how each group approaches a product-purchase decision is a useful one.

The Surprise Package

Moore's *Crossing the Chasm* model is useful in understanding consumer frustration with many electronic products today. As an increasing number of high-tech consumer products come on to the market, more surprise packages are being delivered to unsuspecting customers. A *surprise package* is a term I use to describe an established or fairly stable product concept that's improved in some high-tech way, and now requires unexpected and significant changes in a user's behavior. A good example of this would be a cordless phone. The phone concept is decades old and extremely well established. Ingrained expectations of how the product should behave exist, as well as a lifetime of learned behaviors on how to use it. But, with the new wave of high-tech evolution going on, the cordless phone is now updated with not only cordless technology, but also with built-in answering machines, caller ID, and more. Many of these changes are benign, but others have significant consequences.

As an example, I have two cordless phones in my house. After installing them, my wife was on phone A and she wanted our son to use phone B to pick up the extension. Even though this was something you've been able to do for the last 60 years with normal phones, it was completely impossible with this new phone system. We could only transmit to one handset at a time, so the kids couldn't speak to Grandma at the same time as my wife. She was quite frustrated and rightly so. This product was a significant step backward for her. When faced with purchasing a phone again, my wife was fairly adamant that we couldn't repeat this mistake.

This wasn't a simple technology limitation because the phone was clearly capable of "broadcasting" to all phones in the house at once. When I called the company to ask if it knew of any way around this issue, the representative was quite clear: this was a feature. This company had clearly designed this phone to be like a business phone system where you could have any number of phones and you could transfer calls among them, just as you do at the office. Of course, this phone was sold to homes that would rarely have more than two phones in the entire house. This design decision didn't reflect the likely demographics of the company's purchasing consumers.

Surprise packages, such as my cordless phone, are being created quite frequently today. Companies take product concepts that are now far into the laggard range of stability and established behavior, and they change the product significantly. So much so that the new product is effectively repositioned "back to the front" of the curve, creating a high-tech product that can only be used or appreciated by the forgiving and accomplished early-adopter group of consumers. This is where much of consumer backlash appears, as safely mature and benign products, such as TVs, radios, thermostats, home phones, and even cars are turned back into early adopter products, and then sold to an unsuspecting laggard audience. It's no surprise consumers are in revolt with all these new, digitized products.

The mistake many companies make is they don't appreciate how their products fit on to Moore's Technology Adoption Life Cycle. Disrupting these behaviors with insensitive and complex design is much too easy. What companies need to understand is they aren't only creating a high-tech product for early adopters, but they're also selling into the ultraconservative and easily frustrated laggard group.

Consumer electronic products rarely follow *tent evolution*-slow, steady progress of a stable product concept. Products are changing not only with new features, but with features that reduce the functionality, as seen with the cordless phone example. When creating Simplicity in product design, the established nature of the product category and the user behaviors of the product must be understood or your product will de-evolve, creating a product that feels like it's taking as many steps backward as forward.

THE USER INTERFACE DOESN'T EXIST!

In talking about Simplicity to others, I've found the standard definition of what a user interface is no longer works. We are trapped by the current definition. In fact, I've finally come to the conclusion that user interfaces don't exist. Or, at least, they don't exist in the same way we talk about them. The term *user interface* implies a single object, a bit of code, which represents everything the user can do with a product. This is misleading and dangerous because it limits your thinking, analysis, and planning about how to design a commercial product.

We are in a situation much like George Orwell's famous book, *1984*. In that novel, the government limited the people's vocabulary to reduce their ability to express themselves. We, too, have a limited vocabulary influencing our thinking. We need a richer set of words to enable us greater explorations of problems and solutions. I suggest three separate layers ultimately compose the entire user experience: The Presentation layer, the Task layer, and the Infrastructure layer.

The Presentation Layer

The *Presentation* layer contains the physical, graphic representation of the product, both in hardware and software. The physical case, the push buttons, as well as the onscreen icons and screen layout enable the user to interact with the product. This is what is classically thought of as the user interface. The Presentation layer is primarily graphical in nature and is preoccupied with the presentation of the given functionality of the product.

The Task Layer

The *Task* layer concerns how the user completes tasks when using the device. What is the precise sequence of steps needed to complete a given goal? For example, let's compare desktop e-mail and text messages on mobile phones. Both have a similar goal, which is to receive text messages. The standard desktop e-mail client usually requires 1) configuration of the device, 2) choosing a menu item or a button to start downloading new messages, and 3) opening the Inbox before reading new messages. Mobile phones, on the other hand, automatically configure themselves and alert the user when a new message arrives, offering them the option to open the new arrival immediately. Now, to be fair, e-mail and text messages are different technologies. I don't want to carry this comparison too far but, at a simple-enough level, they do have similar goals, yet different task models.

While no one has done this, you could imagine a text messaging application and an e-mail application with a nearly identical Presentation layer, both showing lists of incoming messages using the same fonts and icons. Yet no one would ever consider them the same program as they would behave in a completely different manner.

The Infrastructure Layer

The Infrastructure layer concerns itself with the underpinnings of the product. What are the enabling factors that allow the product to offer a compelling solution? Just as important are the disabling factors that prevent other solutions from consideration.

In the e-mail versus text-messaging example, the latter's Task layer was much simpler, if more limited. This was due in part to the auto-configuration capability that comes from the GSM phone specification.

This capability is part of the Infrastructure layer because it simply isn't possible for e-mail systems to provide such as service yet. No amount of user interface work will make e-mail systems autoconfigure.

A Car Analogy

An analogy to an automobile might help clarify these layers. A Presentation layer example would be the dashboard, which displays the dials and gauges that not only make the car look nice, but also give information to make decisions. A Task layer example would encompass the steps necessary to start the car. The latest cars literally start at the push of a button but previous models required keys inserted, turned, held in place if not started, but quick release if the car did start. Recall that older cars required a choke to be used in cold weather, making the task even more complicated. If used incorrectly, the car could flood and be unable to start for some time. An Infrastructure layer example would be the internal, technical aspects of the car, which dictated much of the starting sequence. For older cars, there was no option to remove the choke at that time; it had to be there in some form. How it manifested itself to the car owner, whether as a button or a lever, was a Presentation layer detail. With more sophisticated engines and microprocessors it has been possible finally to remove the choke and even the key-turning sequence. Without these innovations, both the Presentation and Task layers were severely restricted.

How This Improves Our Discussion

Many companies only think of the user interface as the Presentation layer. They think of it as a pretty thing that should be added later in the product, after the heavy engineering is complete. Imagine the problems a designer would have working on a car dashboard if he were told that to use the radio, you have to turn off the heater first. Not only that but, if you don't turn off the heater first, you could damage the radio. This sounds a bit absurd when discussing cars, but it happens all the time with computers. Take turning off your computer, for instance. Computers have off switches, but you can't use them unless you first choose Shut Down. To forget this risks corrupting your hard disk.

By having these three layers, discussing the impact of a product decision and how choices exist for fixing it is much easier. For example, limitations in the Infrastructure layer almost always have a big impact on the Task and Presentation layers. Say you have a portable product with a short battery life. You'll probably be forced to put in battery-saving measures, such as requiring the device to go to sleep. This means the user must "wake up" the device before using it, adding to the task load. In addition, this will require changes to the Presentation layer; possibly a battery icon on the screen at all times. Things can get even worse. When the battery goes dead, you might lose or corrupt data, so a need might exist for strange dialog boxes, which might pop up at strange times to warn of impending danger, and so on.

What's important about the previous battery example is that a bad infrastructure problem is hard to fix. You don't want to simply slap up a error dialog box, which lives in the Presentation layer, to fix deep problems with battery life. A bad infrastructure problem also has potentially significant impact on the Task layer, making the product harder to use.

The same interlayer problem occurs with a poor Task layer affecting the Presentation layer. Suppose the product has a bad Task layer design, so the user must complete a complex sequence of steps. Historically, if the user made a misstep, the only design solution considered was to put up a clear and explanatory error dialog box, so the user knows what to do. This Presentation layer fix to a Task layer problem is clearly limited. Fixing a problem in the Task layer is much harder if all you can do is change the Presentation layer. Sometimes, this is your only choice but, usually, it's a poor one.

Whenever this situation occurred at Apple, we called it putting "lipstick on a pig." The HI team was often brought in at the last minute to fix a problem with no ability to change anything technical in the product. Everything had to be done with Presentation layer changes.

Naming these three layers provide a powerful tool. It enable you to discuss problems that exist within a specific layer and analyze solutions within that layer as the first solution to discuss. Breaking down the user interface into these three layers creates a richer vocabulary to discuss and, more important, to manage the creation of good design.

Example: Just a Simple Change to the Menus

Apple had hierarchical menus like most other operating systems, but ours were limited to five levels deep, which seemed reasonable at the time. A software vender came in and asked a colleague of mine to help with his port of a Unix application to the Mac. The problem was his product needed hierarchical menus that went six levels deep. Could we come in and help him fix the interface?

The implication was that changing from six levels to five would be a small change. How hard could it be? This isn't a simple presentation task, though. The reason six levels were there was the Task layer structure of the problem. The product had deep assumptions of how to present information, and to remove a level involved deep changes to the Task layer of the program. Making such a change could never be a quick fix.

Example: Finding Task Problems

Most mobile phones have a lock keypad function. This locks the keypad so presses don't accidentally dial the phone when it's placed in your pocket. Locking the keys at first glance appears to be a Presentation layer problem: How do you show users they can lock the phone, which buttons are pressed, and what is the feedback? It's tempting to think that once you have the feature checked off, you are done with it and you can move on.

But now comes the Task layer and what is required to use the phone for basic tasks. What should happen when the phone rings and the phone is locked? The broader task is answering the phone. Automatically unlocking the phone when a phone call comes in seems reasonable. This is much better than forcing a manual unlock as the phone is ringing. So the phone auto-unlocks when a call is received. So far, so good.

The trouble is only beginning, though. What happens is that people receive phone calls while the phone is in their pockets. If your phone is set on Silent mode for a meeting, you'd never know the call came in or you might even have intentionally ignored it. In either case, you now have an unlocked phone in your pocket and you can freely dial random phone numbers, or worse, speed dial someone and leave them a 15-minute phone message of your meeting, filtered through your pocket fabric.

Notice that this problem is fairly easy to solve. You have only to relock the phone when the call is over. But the lesson here is that new problems can arise by only addressing an issue in the Presentation layer. You usually need to work through the broader tasks in the Task layer to make sure you fully solved all the problems. The first step is in understanding that you need to look beyond the basic interface. The next step is in using the tools to look further. These will be discussed in Chapter 5, "User Blindness."

Example: Technical Architecture Is an Infrastructure Problem

The previous Bluetooth example is a classic problem of infrastructure creating several problems in the Presentation layer. The technical specification for Bluetooth treats all devices as potentially hostile and, as a result, a lengthy set of steps is required to find, authenticate, and connect to a bluetooth device. While there are times when such steps might be necessary, the specifications insistence on treating all devices in this way make it extremely difficult for simple consumer products, such as headsets and phones, to be easily configured and used by your average phone user.

No amount of pretty icons or informative error messages can fix this infrastructure problem. A fix to the overall technology must occur, which will allow the presentation to be much simpler.

This fix can take two forms. The most difficult route is to fix the Bluetooth spec itself. This is the strongest solution, but one that will take much time and energy. The other option is to effectively hack the technology and come up with an bandage, which will make the problem simpler and clear up the presentation problems. A few were discussed earlier, such as limiting the problem to headsets or automatically looking for headsets if one hasn't been set up yet. These are usually the types of solutions that make for breakthrough products as they finesse the problem. This is also discussed in Chapter 9, "Innovation Blindness."

CONCLUSION

Much of the complexity you see in products today is the result of the rapid technological growth, which is unintentionally changing mature products back into "high-tech" products, which only can be mastered by early adopters. Dragging mature and established products back to the beginning of the adoption curve is driving users crazy. This doesn't mean the Moore adoption curve is wrong – it's simply far too easy to move products back to the front of the curve. Either you should make a product super high tech, and then rebrand it as an early adopter product or you must realize it's a laggard product and you make sure you don't fundamentally disrupt the ingrained approach to using it.

One of the first steps in making the Simplicity Shift is understanding you have a problem. If you're selling high-tech products into an established market, you have to make sure you don't assume a market of early adopters. The Simplicity Shift also requires new thinking and new ways of discussing problems. Design isn't only about making pretty icon changes to the Presentation layer. Instead, it's about understanding the Task and Infrastructure layers enough to make the hard trade-offs to achieve Simplicity. The Task and Infrastructure layers are where the true problems lurk. By actively looking at the user experience as something that exists in the Presentation, Task, and Infrastructure layers, you have a means of discussing how your product can develop and meet consumer needs.

Design Break: The GPRS Study

The purpose of these Design Breaks is to give you some real-life examples and exercises to clarify the points discussed in this book. I find the problem with examples is the most meaty and insightful ones are viciously complex and need far too much background to be practical. I hope I found a middle ground, showing products of enough depth that aren't overwhelming in detail.

This first example is more of a sad story than a design exercise, but it's, unfortunately, typical of how early strategic planning can fail. If the strategy is wrong, getting a well-designed product is nearly impossible. Subsequent Design Breaks will be more hands-on — taking an existing product and reworking it using the tools in the book.

THE PROBLEM

At one company where I worked, my team was putting together a design for a GPRS phone. GPRS, like most of the technologies in the mobile phone industry, is a richly technical function that almost seems to create more problems for the user than the solutions it offers. In principle, GPRS is supposed to allow high-speed data access to the phone, so you can browse the Web at much higher speeds than before. Not only that, but you can always be online instead of the old-fashioned modem style approach where you have to dial in. This dialing process could take up to a minute and, with GPRS, it was to be nearly instantaneous.

The industry was touting GPRS as the next savior of the phone industry and my company was putting it into every product it sold. My design team knew this was going to be a problem because even a casual look at the technical specifications showed numerous exceptions and problems that "had to be brought to the user's attention." These words are almost always a bad sign.

The programming team was under considerable time pressure – a common situation in high-tech companies. We approached them to help design the product and were told, politely, they had to get this out quickly and didn't have time for a complete user-interface design. They would get the technology out quickly, and then fix it up in a later release. Clearly, they considered user-centered design a luxury that could easily be lived without, which was a decision that came back to haunt them. We proceeded with our design work anyway because we could see this was going to be a problem that wouldn't go away.

ANALYSIS

We formed a small team to put together some user Scenarios (this is discussed in more detail in Chapter 5). We didn't focus on the obvious, high-end features such as high-speed web browsing but, instead, focused on the more basic activities that covered everyday issues, such as roaming out of coverage or going into a tunnel. All we wanted to do was to make the impact of this new technology on the average user obvious by walking through these simple tasks. We were trying to make sure everyone understood and interpreted the technical specification consistently.

Our deliverable was simple: a fairly short slide presentation showing each Scenario and what questions came up as we were looking at them. For example, if you were downloading a long e-mail and went into a tunnel, would the users have to deal with an error, what type of error would this be, and how would they then recover when they came out of the tunnel? We sent this slide show off to the GPRS experts.

DISCOVERY 1 – THEY DIDN'T KNOW

The first and most surprising result was the technical architects couldn't answer our basic questions! We were all surprised that such simple issues had little common agreement. Our slide show prompted questions that hadn't even been asked yet. We got different answers from different teams. When we pointed this out to them, there was clear confusion. There was a flurry of e-mails clarifying our questions and the proposed solutions. Then we had a teleconference, where everyone came together to discuss all these issues at the same time.

What didn't help was our Scenarios were fairly nontechnical. We spoke the nomenclature of the user, not that of the GPRS specification. This sometimes created misunderstandings for the technical team because our terms were too soft and vague for them. We solved this problem by walking through the Scenario and clarifying any vague statements until the loose ends were resolved. Eventually, we figured out what was supposed to happen and what errors were going to occur. We had to become much more technical than we had planned, but it was the only way to bridge the communication divide between us and the experts. In effect, we had to speak two languages to be understood.

Notice we weren't attempting design at this stage. We were only trying to understand how that product was meant to be used in a few common situations. Even this simple analytic task was extremely difficult to complete because getting a consensus was a complex communication exercise.

The inability of the technical teams to know answers to some of these basic user situations was surprising. This demonstrates how many project managers think only about the big picture issues of shiny new technology. Problems such as errors were considered details to be worked out later. Our slide show forced a realization that these were deep questions with messy technical answers, which were critical to resolve for the product.

DISCOVERY 2 – IT WASN'T ALL NEEDED

The second discovery was that the GPRS specification was huge. Our team of programmers was diligently implementing the entire standard. The problem with most technical standards, especially for something as complex as GPRS, is the lack of any priority. The GPRS spec was simply a long list of functional calls required to be implemented.

Only one problem existed – our slide show revealed that substantial sections of this specification weren't required. Once we worked through the basic Scenarios, it was clear that many corners of the spec weren't needed for the type of handsets we were building. Once we had a better idea of how the phone was to be used, there was a clear version 1 subset we would need to get the basic product out and a version 2 subset, which would be much more complete for more high-end phones in the future.

This, too, was a shocking discovery because this was a tightly scheduled project. We had little time to get this product out to market, yet here was the programming team implementing most of the spec, when some of its difficult and time-consuming subsets could have been removed.

DISCOVERY 3 – DEEP PROBLEMS SURFACED

The third discovery was we uncovered problems no one had anticipated: you can't have "always-on" web access. The details are fairly low level but, to give you a rough idea, it became clear that the specification didn't handle communication well between applications. It wasn't well understood how two applications could use the GPRS data channel at the same time. So, while you could have always-on web access, you might never receive your e-mail. This issue was much more complex than described but, overall, this was a huge step down from the vision of what GPRS could be.

CONCLUSION

The results from this study created some rather unfortunate and nasty high-level marketing problems, which had a visible impact on the product. The company had to go to our customers and explain that we weren't going to have always-on web access in version 1, why, and when we were going to deliver it next. This was a politically messy situation.

This all came from a four-week study. Unfortunately, with many technology innovations, the obvious benefits are clear, but the actual path to get these benefits isn't well understood. Yet products seem to forge ahead, regardless. This is not only a bad idea from the user design point-of-view, it's also disastrous from a software architecture point-of-view.

The power of this example is in how clearly it demonstrates that user interface issues have a fundamental impact not only on the Presentation layer and the Infrastructure layer, but on business strategy as well. Because this type of analysis deeply affects the product concept, it must happen before development work starts. This is especially true because this type of work is fairly fast, inexpensive, and usually saves product development time.

A more political issue was how "back door" our approach had to be. The project management team didn't want our help and, unfortunately, we were in a situation where we forged ahead anyway. It shouldn't come as a surprise that the results of our study weren't acted on immediately. You can't force this type of report on people. This is why I push so hard that the Simplicity Shift is a cultural change in the company. This type of report must be required by management so it's supported and, more importantly, acted on, when completed.

This is a strong example of how Simplicity and good design must come from within the culture of a company and not be imposed from behind by a design department. Mature companies understand that design is a strategic input to any product process. It must be done early and discussed at all levels of the product process. If the company doesn't have that culture, it's hard to break through. This is why this book is targeted to managers even more than designers.

5 | User Blindness

*If one is master of one thing and understands one thing
well, one has at the same time, insight into and
understanding of many things.*

—*van Gogh*

INTRODUCTION

When designing any consumer product, some target user is always in
mind, whether conscious or unconscious, to help guide your decisions.
Making any product decision is difficult if you don't have some idea of
who will be using it. The problem is this target user is a difficult person
to know with any certainty. Many companies design a product that
seems reasonable, without any real attempt to uncover more information
about actual target users. What often happens in companies that don't
do active user research is the companies base their concept of who the
user is on one of two equally invalid stereotypes. The first is a user who
reflects the company culture – a person "just like them." It shouldn't
be surprising to know this person is competent and in need of many
advanced features in the product. The second stereotype is motivated
by marketing concerns. So many potential customers exist that what
ends up being the target is a conglomeration of all possible users. This
creates an impossibly demanding multiuser, who requires every possible
feature from the product.

Both stereotypes prevent you from seeing the actual user and what
he will need from your product. User blindness comes from thinking

you know who the user is. You're blinded because you already have a stereotype in mind, so you don't bother to look any further.

Where user blindness costs the most is when the concept of the user isn't clear or shared across the product team. Marketing tends to target as many users as possible; each feature is as important as the next. Development tends to target users who are just like themselves, applying common sense ideas that usually aren't. By designing for everyone, you get a confused product. By designing for the obvious user, you create a high-end product and lose the larger customer. By inadvertently trying to create a product designed for both of these extremes, the situation is nearly impossible. Finding true Simplicity is hard. To achieve it, everyone must be clear on precisely who the target user is.

Many techniques, from focus groups to ethnographic studies, give you a deeper understanding and help to identify your target user. Even more, these types of studies can give you key observations into their work flow patterns and daily frustrations, both of which can be inspirational when planning new product concepts.

Even though these techniques have been around for years, they still don't seem to make the type of impact they're capable of and, in my experience, two broad reasons exist for this: naiveté and lost understanding. *Naiveté* is usually found in small companies just starting to consider the user interface. They don't have the experience or the resources to tackle a proper design job. Fairly in-depth activities, such as an ethnographic study, appear risky because of up-front costs. Over time, as the companies mature, these costs will be seen as good investments. But when a young company is just starting up, it's often better to begin small and use simple tools to get the team communicating and sharing a user concept before working on studies that explore the user model more deeply.

Lost understanding comes from more mature companies that have a design department. In this case, the company does some type of probing user research and deep understanding is found. The problem here lies not in the results, but in the communication of the results. The research does, indeed, inform the design, but only internally, to the design team itself. Unfortunately, the research doesn't inform the broader company's thinking. All too common in these mature companies is to take a well-researched product design, and then hobble it by having other departments, which don't share this deeper understanding, make inconsistent product decisions that countermand the original design. Examples of these decisions would be dropped features or changes in the hardware specification.

Naiveté is the easier of the two to fix because some fairly easy tools exist to get a company thinking outside its old engineering ways. Lost understanding is the more difficult problem to solve because the company is doing investigative work, but it doesn't seem to seep into the broader companywide decision making.

Curing user blindness is a two-step process: the first step is making an attempt at getting a clearer picture of the target user and the second step is incorporating this information into the product process. This clarity places your company in a much stronger position. You have the understanding and the power to remove things from the product that aren't going to affect it. This can save enormous amounts of time, development costs, and emotional anguish.

This chapter lays out two Insights that address this blindness. The first Insight is the use of *Personas*, which breaks up the multiusers into a few precise and detailed customers. The second insight, *Scenarios*, is a technique to walk through these new Personas, so you can understand what aspect of the product is critical to them.

I've found that using only these tools, as simple as they are, provides an effective communications framework to discuss and negotiate product decisions. These tools aren't meant to replace the classic deep user-study techniques, such as focus groups and ethnographic studies, but are, instead, a bridge into using them. A company has to start thinking, discussing, and creating a consensus about the user before it makes use of studies that provide a deeper insight.

INSIGHT 1 – PERSONAS: BREAK UP THE MULTIUSER

What It Is

Personas are a simple tool that breaks up your multiuser into smaller pieces. Personas are nothing more than a detailed description of a person who will use your product. This description doesn't talk about features, time to market, or your company in any way. It only talks about specific, individual people. This description is fairly short – no more that a sheet of paper – with a reasonable description of who this customer is and enough about that customer to know how he or she would approach using your product.

Why It's Important

The problem with user blindness is it assumes everything is important to a multiuser and any discussion is focused on a long list of the features a multiuser will need. Personas create a specific target person, someone with a name and some details that fleshes them out and makes them real. Designing for a Persona makes you walk through the specifics of the product for that person and this exercise forces out issues you'd hadn't been able to see before. At its best, the Persona is a tool to make you slow down and walk through a character, forcing you to realize many little things that are clearly important, but never make it on to any feature list.

Example

I was in a product meeting discussing how to rework the way messages were sent and received for a new consumer phone concept. The design was vastly simpler than existing desktop e-mail clients and removed many of the more high-end features. We had created a Persona called Emma, which was a young teenage consumer and had an established use pattern based on our knowledge of current SMS messages. This wasn't a complex model but, by giving the characterization a name and some details, we could focus our discussions.

What's critical to this example is that Emma was agreed to by everyone in the meeting before we started. When we started getting bogged down in a particularly powerful feature, which some wanted to keep and others wanted to remove, I said, "We're not designing this for us. We're designing this for Emma. Do you think she would be upset by this decision?" The answer was clearly no and we were able to move on.

This shows how Personas are usually more powerful in slimming down a product, rather than amplifying it. In this meeting, all sorts of crazy high-end features were being discussed, but it was clear that Emma couldn't or wouldn't use any of them.

In this case we were able to throw away a feature completely, which isn't always so simple. Sometimes, you must have certain features because political or marketing pressures require their inclusion. By having Emma as a touch stone, however, this gives you perspective. If it turns out these required features are of no use to Emma, you can then approach these features differently. Placing them into the product – possibly off to the side – in a way that doesn't affect Emma so strongly. This is discussed in more detail in the Chapter 7.

How to Get Them – Field Studies

The user-centered design community has a long and successful history in getting Personas. This usually involves field studies or focus groups. Field studies focus on watching users doing their jobs, using an existing product and observing the problems, key tasks, and insights into how users go about their work. Focus groups tend to bring people together in an attempt to get the same information from an open question-and-answer session. These types of research not only create Personas, but they also create findings that help focus your product concept and product positioning.

Every time I complete one of these studies, I feel it has returned rich dividends and has always been worth it. These studies are most valuable when you're creating a completely new type of product with a fairly complex marketing concept where you need a solid understanding of the consumers to make sure you're delivering the right solution.

Another advantage to these studies is they uncover big deep issues and inform you of concerns that you had no idea existed previously. There's no substitute for this type of research and I always recommend these types of studies when you need this level of understanding.

How to Get Them – The Cheap Way

You don't always need this level of understanding, though. Many companies have an existing product line and they're trying to improve a device that is being cost reduced. These are fairly focused tasks within well-defined domains. In these situations, the design doesn't need deep field insights as much as it needs product clarification.

In addition, field studies can be expensive. While this money usually is repaid many times over, small companies simply don't have the money to consider this type of work for every project. At times, a smaller tool can deliver nearly the same understanding without the up-front costs.

When you're in a more focused situation, you can create Personas in a more low-key manner. Just as many marketing departments often have a range of target users, you can create a range of Personas that cover expected users. The trap is in trying to create a completely representative cross section. This isn't a segmentation study, where you break up all users into a full topology of user types. The goal of this insight is to break up the multiuser into a few real people who will give you a detailed consideration of how they would use the product.

Here's a list of information I'd try to capture in a Persona: name, age, marital status, number of children and their ages, job, how they get to work, primary activities outside work, and a photograph. A photograph is important because it turns this flat description into a real person – something which you can relate to more easily. It's easy to find a photo of someone reasonable on the Internet.

Then, depending on what the product is, I'd ask lifestyle questions that help understand how the person might use the product. In the case of Personas used for phone design, we described the common calling patterns of a person, who in their life they called, and when they called.

This might seem like a simplistic approach, but I find that asking these questions of a group elicits strong responses. Instead of working from a high-end user down, these types of questions, as you go through them, tend to build a Persona from scratch. Answering the lifestyle questions that reflect how this person will need the product is a sobering experience. You simply can't create one person who will need everything and this becomes obvious when you try to put the Persona on paper. This is the power of this simple tool. By writing it down, you immediately face realistic expectations of what one person can do.

Grabbing "real" people and asking them the same questions is also possible. This can be done in all sorts of sneaky ways, such as grabbing

Grant

•Who he is...
- •32 years old, sales representative
- •Married, one son, small house in Guilford
- •Extended family around Machester area
- •Owns a Ford Mondeo
- •Enjoys Formula 1
- •Plans long weekend getaways with family

•Technology use
- •Moderate day phone user, bill paid for by employer
  - •heavy **work** voice mail, moderate mobile voicemail
- •Light text user, moderate fax user
- •Heavy Web/e-mail user
  - •Corporate account
  - •Personal Yahoo account
- •Heavy PC user at work
  - •Also at home (web surfing/digital photos)
- •Has a Palm
- •Has 100+ names in phone book

•Key goals
- •Be instantly available during work hours
- •Get information while on the move
- •Stay in touch with family and friends

FIGURE 5-1. Sample Persona.

people who call in on tech-support lines or in store visits. Remember, you're definitely not getting a statistically valid sample of who your user is. You're simply exploring real people and getting enough details so these people have enough depth to help you understand what might motivate their behaviors. Figure 5.1 shows a sample Persona I used in one of my projects.

How to Do It

Many times when I've introduced Personas, there's a "you've got to be kidding" feeling around the room. Breaking up the target audience into more precise groups makes sense to most, but the large number of unnecessary details makes some programmers laugh out loud. I'll admit, discussing whether Clifford the bartender has three or four kids can seem a bit surreal at times.

The goal is to create a range of Personas, discuss them, and then find those that represent a reasonable target for the product. This is best done by the product team as a group, not only the designers. Having the designers create several sample Personas first as straw men works well. Then you can have the product team review this list. By "product team," I mean, at least have people from marketing, development, sales, and design. If this is a large team, it needn't be everyone, but have a representative from each team. If you don't have the team's buy in, you'll constantly be revisiting issues because you won't have shared assumptions in the team decision making.

This review group needs to run through the sample Personas and decide if they make sense. New Personas might even be added. Once this is done, you must rank the Personas. Start with approximately six Personas, and then come up with two, and only two. I must repeat that these two Personas won't represent the majority of your market. What you want to do is to find a reasonable subset that will clarify common use patterns of the product.

The majority of this exercise is having the product team discussing the Personas. This gets the power user out of the blood of many in the team. Just having this discussion does wonders to help people realize the range of potential users. This encourages sensitivity in the entire team, hence, my insistence that much of the team be involved. The Personas will have additional use in Insight 2: Scenarios.

Shared Culture

I know working through a product concept for a retired woodworker named Earl sounds odd, but in understanding that Earl does exist, you can start using your product through his eyes. What you end up doing is creating a shared understanding by your product team of what Earl represents.

Personas are most powerful when they're placed up on the wall with a big picture of Earl at the top. This poster becomes a token, an embodiment of an approach to the product. Hundreds of times, decisions must be made by individual members of the team. "What would Earl do?" or "What does Earl need here?" are the types of questions you hear when teams have taken Personas on board.

What this all boils down to is creating a shared culture. Earl represents a key customer. Earl's Persona is detailed enough that people feel he exists and makes the decisions of the team have real consequences. This, in turn, makes the team sensitive, assessing the impact of any particular decision.

This is one reason making up a Persona is almost as good as using a professional focus group. As long as this Persona is precise, realistic, and shared by the team, it will create a culture of how decisions should be made for this product.

Objection: Personas Are too Specific

At first, people resist using Personas because they appear so focused and not representative of the broader consumer base. The concern is that designing for only this one person is much too constraining. If Emma, for example, is a horse trainer, are you really going to add a feature to the product that will work only for horse lovers? Clearly not but then, why, the argument goes, do we care if Emma is a horse trainer?

The point here is to create a detailed person who appears real. By making Emma a horse trainer, you imagine a product that could be used while riding a horse. This might mean the product must be sensitive to being used on the move. This has value to a hiker or a delivery boy, as well, but you might never have considered mobile use unless you'd imaged Emma in the first place. Personas start you down a path of more sensitive thinking.

Getting past this minority problem is difficult. Everyone would feel so much better if a "majority" Persona could be created, but that rarely exists. If the Personas are picked carefully, however, they'll represent a cloud of other Personas that will have similar needs. By building a product that's perfect for Earl, you're almost, by definition, making it good for this cloud.

Objection: Two Is too Few

If two Personas are good, aren't five better? This is a tempting line of reasoning, but it's poorly motivated. The goal isn't to cover the customer base but, instead, to focus. You can't focus with five Personas. The pressure to have many more Personas will come as the product team tries to narrow the list. This is difficult to do because choosing only two means you must value one Persona over another. This might bring out a little tension in the group. It's so much easier on the team to let all five Personas go through.

By starting with approximately six Personas and narrowing it to two, you're forcing the team to make shared decisions. I guarantee this team activity will create lively debate as the underlying beliefs of each team come tumbling out. This won't be easy because people in general are civil and don't have the energy to come to terms with these deep differences. But these differences will be relived every day of the project unless the team works through them. Getting down to two Personas will be a communication achievement that will go a long way in making the team pull in the same direction.

INSIGHT 2 – SCENARIOS: WALK IN THEIR SHOES

What It Is

Scenarios are much like Personas and they're a simple concept. A Scenario is a short description of what a Persona wants to accomplish, such as contacting a friend or checking the weather. One critical aspect of Scenarios is they're focused on a Persona, trying to accomplish a task using their words and their world. A Scenario isn't to "download e-mails into the inbox," but to "check for messages from the office." This might sound unnecessarily picky, but by focusing on the broader issue, you realize that context drives much more insight than you might first imagine.

Take the example of checking messages. For certain Personas, the case might be they don't get many messages and downloading e-mails would usually result in nothing. Those Personas would prefer a system that notified them when a message arrived, so they wouldn't have to waste time needlessly checking their e-mail. This is one of the reasons the original WebTV set-up box had a small LED, which would blink when new e-mail arrived. The way you ask the question forms the answer you will find.

Why It Is Important

One consequence of user blindness is this: without a shared understanding of who the target user will be, all features appear to have equal weight. This creates complexity because you can't layer your design. Every feature is important, so everything gets placed in front of the user at once. This usually creates a cluttered and complex design.

I agree that more sophisticated users do have more demanding tasks than novice users, but an even more insightful truth is that all users usually have the same core tasks. By discovering these core tasks, you have your first design priorities set in front of you. Design for these priorities first and you'll find Simplicity in your design is significantly easier. Start here and the rest will follow.

Another consequence of user blindness is this: with all features apparently equal, only the flashy high-tech features tend to get any attention. The product puts far too much weight on features that might rarely be used. This was discussed previously in Chapter 4's example about GPRS. By using Scenarios, we could break down the large flashy technology into smaller pieces, finding problems with some and removing the need for others altogether. The feature itself is fairly uninspiring. The user's tasks that require this feature are much more insightful.

How to Do It

Just like Personas, established tools, such as field studies or ethnographic studies, can discover what Scenarios are important. These are the types of Scenarios you probably wouldn't know on your own. These discoveries are useful because they uncover ways your product is needed that might not be at all obvious.

Just as a simple way exists to create Personas, a simple way also exists to create Scenarios. This won't have the deeper impact that would come from field work, but it can still be effective. This also has the advantage of being fast and inexpensive to create.

The basic place to start is to create the obvious Scenarios, such as turning on the device or using it for basic tasks. If it's a microwave, cook something. If it's a digital timer, imagine where it would be and give it a realistic thing to time. The purpose with this fairly quick Scenario isn't to uncover a new and ground-breaking use but, instead, to take fairly obvious uses of the product and place them in context with a Persona.

In the GPRS example, we were trying to expose task problems, so we took about twelve basic tasks that were currently possible with existing mobile phones, such as downloading e-mail or going into a tunnel. These Scenarios tested whether these same tasks still worked with the new technology.

Where Scenarios are most powerful is in uncovering problems. By taking fairly boring tasks and working through a Persona, you uncover aspects of the product that weren't apparent before. By having a detailed Persona walk through the Scenario, the surrounding context becomes more apparent. So, instead of setting the microwave to cook for ten seconds, you have David thawing a bagel before he catches the bus. Scenarios try to capture not only the product action, but also the environment in which that action is being performed.

As another example, I was working on a design for a mobile phone that had a stylus for tapping on the screen. The Scenario was simple – nothing more than reading a new message that had arrived. For this Persona, however, they happened to be on a bus going to work. In imagining them using this product with a small screen and a small stylus while on a crowded bus, it wasn't hard to determine this could

---

Scenario 8: GPRS Suspension

Persona: David

Prerequisites: David is online with the WAP browser
                      using GPRS to connect. A phone call comes in
                      while he's browsing

Setting the scene: While checking football scores, David
                      receives a phone call from a friend
                      regarding the trip they are about to make.
                      David takes the call, talks briefly on the
                      phone, and then hangs up. He then continues
                      to use the browser to read the rest of the
                      match details.

FIGURE 5-2. Sample Scenario.

be inconvenient to many people, not only to this Persona. This helped us understand that for this product, using core functions of the phone without requiring the stylus would be useful. This started us down a long path of questioning the value of the stylus and how to consider designing basic tasks without requiring its use.

Example: GPRS

Figure 5-2 shows a sample Scenario that came from the GPRS work discussed earlier in the book.

In this particular case, the Scenario was fairly specific and short. Note how it carefully calls out the prerequisites, so the technical people reviewing it have a good idea of the phone state when this Scenario takes place.

This might seem like a trivial little paragraph, but it brought the house down when we worked through it. By forcing the technical team to answer how this was going to work, we exposed many problems and misunderstandings about the product.

Problems

Scenarios are best at taking fairly standard tasks and bringing out the issues that complicate their execution. This is a powerful technique in combating complexity because these observations will enable you to fix problems early in the product cycle.

A common problem in creating the Scenarios is that they aren't generic enough. It's much too easy to say "Download e-mails" rather than "Check for messages from the office." The rewording is important because it breaks free of the existing product concept. One trick to doing this is to go ahead and use the established or technical name for the feature, and then rewrite it without using any of these words. Look to the Persona to give you some inspiration. "Download" becomes "check" and "e-mail" becomes "messages." Placing the task in context also helps, so I also added "from the office." This might seem a bit frivolous, but by disengaging from your preconceived terms, you create more creative space to work in.

Another problem comes from trying to make the Scenarios too complex. Don't try to "set up an e-mail filter." Start with the basic tasks, such as checking messages, and work them through. Go after Simplicity first. The simple tasks must be tackled because they're the ones that create the biggest design win if you can make a significant improvement in their presentation or use.

PUTTING THESE INSIGHTS TOGETHER

These insights produce a drastically different means of creating a product concept. The first insight – Personas – focuses the team on particular users with specific needs, not those needs of the team. This is a dramatic shift in sensitivity and creative thinking. It also fosters a shared understanding throughout the project and enables individuals to make decisions that support rather than work against, the product design.

The second insight – Scenarios – walks you through the basic tasks for each Persona and force understanding of how they would use the product. This usually uncovers significant opportunities and trouble spots early in the product process.

I like to think of these insights as the "Homework" insights. They help to research and understand the product space. They won't give you a design, but they do soften you up, opening new ways of thinking about the product and uncovering big problems you hadn't seen before.

In addition, these homework assignments produce tangible results that can be shared with the entire team, including management. You can imagine questions like "Have you verified your Personas with marketing?" or "Has that Scenario uncovered an architecture risk?" These two insights break the mystery of the design process and start sharing it with the entire company.

Finally, these insights are fairly fast and inexpensive. A company of any size should be able to pull this off in a few weeks and this is time that can save you trouble down the line.

Once a company is capable of using these simple and fast tools, it can them move up to the more in-depth methods of understanding users, such as ethnographic studies, focus groups, and field studies. These are all effective tools. Recommended books are in the Appendix at the back of the book. These tools are most effective, though, after you have the basic tools in place. You must start working on the communication and agreement of Personas and Scenarios before you can absorb and use the information you find from these deeper tools.

Design Break: Microwave Oven

Out of intense complexities, intense simplicities emerge.
—Winston Churchill

This Design Break is an example of dragging products back to the front of Moore's technology adoption curve. Something simple and reasonably well understood, by the addition of new technology, can become unusable and irritating. Using our new vocabulary, this shows how what appears to be a simple presentation layer problem also has large task-level problems.

Let's start with a "bad" microwave and, by using a Persona and a few Scenarios, we can prioritize the design to reflect the key tasks. By identifying these top tasks, the design almost takes care of itself. This shows how most of the hard work in design is in the up-front thinking. Once you prune away extra, distracting functionality, what's left is fairly easy to mold into a simple and easy to use product.

There are three stages to this Design Break. I begin with the basic task and design just for that task. I then layer on the additional tasks, keeping the spirit of the previous stage. The idea is to make your way through all the features, but to layer them in a way that keeps the simple core of the first stage intact.

PROBLEM

The microwave oven seems so simple: put in food, turn it on, and, finally, take out hot food. The early microwaves were about that simple. Their design was modeled on conventional ovens and they were straightforward to use: Turn a dial to the time you wanted, open the door, stick in the food, and close the door. The oven started automatically. Some units had a special "advanced feature," a power dial, which enables you to set the power at Low, Medium, or High, which provided flexibility for thawing food. Even that was straightforward and not at all hard to understand or use.

Now along comes the digital revolution and cost cutters. Analog timers are both expensive and more likely to require service. The solution offered is a digital timer. They work forever, can be sealed behind protective plastic, and are a fraction of the cost of the original analog dial. This would typically be seen as nothing but a Presentation layer problem because the tasks, which were so straightforward before, are still the same. The assumption is that by replacing an analog dial with a digital timer, the impact will be minor.

To make this concrete, let me introduce an example of a digital timer microwave, as shown in Figure 6-1.

This product has a lot going on. It doesn't reflect simply a small change to a digital timer. This is an example of how products, once they do move to digital interface styles, start sprouting extra features because the addition of an extra button is such a small incremental cost. The presentation layer is now significantly more complex – it isn't even obvious how to turn on the machine. You must look at all the buttons and their double labels to determine which buttons you *aren't* going to use.

What makes this design especially difficult to understand is the smaller buttons on the left aren't buttons at all, but only decorative labels. By pushing the SuperCook button in the upper-right corner, a number appears on the screen that corresponds to the mode you're selecting, 1 for Roast Beef/Lamb, 2 for Roast Pork, and so forth.

This is a good example of an initially simple device category that was once easy to use and fairly well understood by the laggard type of consumer. By adding this digital interface and letting it grow too far, it has been repositioned from the laggard side of the adoption curve back to the front as an innovator type of product. Users of a certain high-tech class can work their way through this design, but the vast majority of consumers will not.

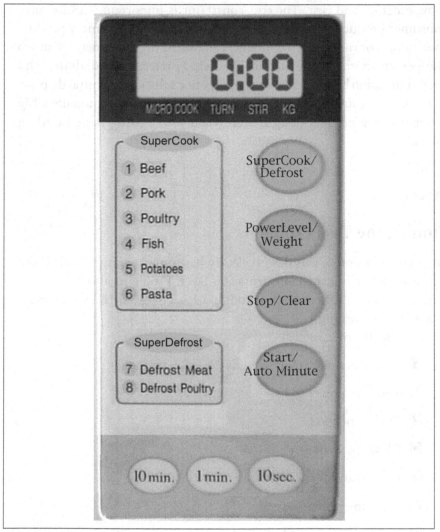

FIGURE 6-1. Example of a digital microwave oven.

The purpose of this Design Break isn't to poke fun at this microwave. Much more important are the generic issues it demonstrates that pervade many modern consumer products. Two such examples illustrated here are poorly designed digital timers and confusing button placement. This Design Break is meant to be a practical example. The goal is not only to improve this design, but also to keep approximately the same function and cost. The cost constraint is important because most consumer product companies have cost reduction as a primary product motivator. For the sake of argument, I'll assume digital timers are much cheaper and more reliable than analog dials. I prefer analog dials in such a design situation because they're a far-superior solution to digital displays with tiny buttons. Besides, it's liberating to know you can make a big difference in a product design, even when you're using basic building blocks.

Analysis

Finding the Task Problems

As previously noted, this design clearly has some layout problems, but this is only looking at the Presentation layer. Problems also exist at the Task layer as well. Let's walk through a basic task, such as thawing a bagel in the morning.

Analog Microwave:

- Turn the timer to 30 seconds

- Turn the power to low

- Put in the food

- Close the door

- Press Start

Digital Timer Microwave:

- Tap the 10-second button three times to get 30 seconds

- Tap the Power/Level button four times (to cycle down from 100 percent power to 70 percent power to 50 percent power to 30 percent power)

- Put in the food

- Close the door

- Press Start

This is a big change. Setting the time is clearly more tedious with the digital buttons, but this isn't an outrageous problem. This is an interaction style that's, unfortunately, becoming more accepted today. The serious problem is with the power setting. By having only a single button, the users must understand that to set the power level, they must press it repeatedly, cycling through various power values. If they go too far, they must keep pressing the button, cycling all the way around. This is not only difficult to use but, more important, it's hard to discover.

In addition to the power button problem, a larger task problem exists when you try to vary the steps slightly. If you open the door first, the buttons don't work. If you try to adjust the power first, the buttons don't work. If half-way through cooking, you need to add a little more time, the time buttons are dead. The previously described steps are the only possible order to follow in starting the unit to cook.

These types of task problems can make for disastrous consequences. For example, once you start cooking, the only way to make a change is to 1) close the door and 2) press Clear. Then you're allowed to start over. When you're cooking on low power, it's easy to forget that pressing Clear resets the power back up to High. If you want to defrost a little more, you accidentally end up cooking your food to a crisp.

Dragging you through the details of this design might sound tedious, but this type of problem is, unfortunately, indicative of many consumer products today. Understanding this puts you in a much stronger position to design your own products properly. The Presentation layer is clearly a problem, but the Task layer problems have the biggest consequences.

Feature Pollution

I previously noted the apparent buttons on the left side of the panel were nothing more than labels. These labels are an attempt to fix a Task layer problem with a Presentation layer fix. The feature in question is SuperCook, which tries to automate some cooking tasks for the consumer. By pushing this, the numerous choices that need to be made force the user to interact with the numerical display. You have to select the number that corresponds to the automated cooking you want. Each press of the SuperCook button changes the number, cycling through all eight types. You also need to select additional parameters by pressing the other buttons on the right. Going into too much detail would be a bit tedious, but I hope you clearly see how trying to use such a limited choice of buttons is a large Task level problem. The attempt to fix the problem was simply to put some pretty labels on the front of the device, a Presentation level solution. This, of course, created further problems because now the labels themselves look like buttons and complicate the design even further.

In addition, this is a classic example of showing too many features to the user at once, or what is commonly called *featuritis*. The primary motivation for this feature was most likely as a marketing tool to differentiate this device from the other low-end microwaves on the showroom floor. It was clearly not from a deep understanding of what typical microwave users need. You can't tell this from the black-and-white photo of the figure, but the SuperCook buttons are a shade of green, while the remaining buttons are gray. This calls the user's primary attention to SuperCook. While this further substantiates the marketing motivation as the device is actively accentuating a high-end feature, it makes the Start button even harder to find. Marketing-driven design may help a product promote itself, but it rarely helps the basic usage of the device.

Persona/Scenarios

Before we start designing, we have to do our homework. Let's begin with a simple Persona:

Fred
Single, sales clerk, age 25, commutes to work on the bus, has friends over frequently. Doesn't like to cook and eats prepared foods, such as TV dinners, microwave popcorn, and bagels from the freezer.

Scenarios:

Basic: Heating microwave pizza for dinner
Advanced: Thawing a bagel for breakfast

While this Scenario is extremely simple, it will be enough for us to make some headway. It might seem a bit odd talking about a guy who takes the bus, but I'm creating a specific character to work through our choices. Imagining Fred in the morning trying to catch the bus isn't hard. Fred's in a hurry, thinking about his day, and he doesn't want his microwave to slow him down.

Fred is also the kind of guy who seems to do basic stuff. You won't see him cooking Veal Cordon Bleu in his microwave. He seems like the perfect guy to be using a low-end microwave.

But even this simple beginning starts us thinking through Fred's schedule. Further questions come to mind that can help improve the Scenario. What other types of food does Fred tend to cook? Do they make a mess inside the oven? How easy is it to clean? Is the oven large enough? Do the foods Fred cooks turn out well in the microwave? Even with this basic Persona/Scenario combination, the questions come tumbling out.

In a professional situation, these questions would be discussed with the product team, including marketing research, if it exists. Many of these questions would already have well-known answers. To make this Design Break a reasonable length, I'm going to assume the previous Persona/Scenario is acceptable, even though it would normally have more detail and discussion. There would also be another Persona to capture a different type of user. But, with this as a given, we'll now walk through the basic and advanced Scenarios as a test of this microwave design.

Approach

So, let's roll up our sleeves and begin. The first step is getting our tasks straight. The first Scenario – heating a microwave pizza for dinner – seems straightforward. This looks like it only involves setting the time and starting the oven. We could also discuss how to improve the microwave's pizza cooking capability by having a rotating plate, a better cooking surface, and so on, but these are outside the scope of this Design Break. We're going to focus only on the panel.

The second Scenario, thawing a bagel for breakfast, is a little trickier. At the implementation level, we're only adding a power level setting, but looking through Fred's eyes can help see a little more. This is breakfast time, it's in the morning, Fred is tired, and he's probably in a hurry to catch the bus. He could easily push the wrong button or accidentally cook the bagel on High, turning it to rubber. This suggests Fred needs a simple power-level setting. Some type of strong visual feedback would also be good, so Fred can be sure what he set is what he's getting.

Now that we have our basic Scenarios, we can consider a new design. Remember, we aren't going to design the entire microwave. We've identified some clear core tasks and we're going to design only for those. This will intentionally avoid other more advanced features. By focusing on designing for only the most basic tasks, finding a simple design, one that will be easy to understand and use, becomes much easier.

Stage 1

The initial design focuses only on the first Scenario and we don't need much to make this happen. Fred simply needs to set the time and start the oven. Setting the time is fairly fixed by our constraints. We have a digital display and buttons to set the time. Given this limitation, the existing button design seems quite reasonable. By having three buttons — one for ten minutes, one for one minute, and one for ten seconds — Fred could quickly set the approximate times needed for microwave cooking.

This makes the design job fairly simple. Figure 6-2 shows the initial design.

Setting the Time on Top
With the task clear, we can incorporate a task flow into the design, set the time, and start the oven. By grouping the time buttons with the

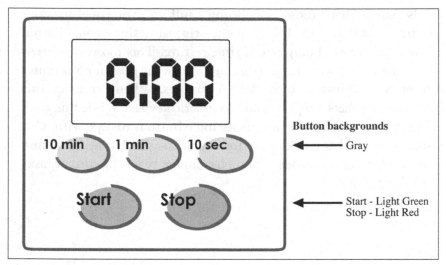

FIGURE 6-2. Stage 1 design.

display, it more closely ties their use with feedback. The button under the display changes the display – this is now much more clear. Once this is set, the task flow then leads you to the Start button, which is just below the Time buttons.

This is a different layout from the original, which had the Time buttons on the bottom and the display at the top. Tying them together like this makes the design much clearer and sets up a vertical flow to use the machine.

Grouping Time with Color-Coded Start/Stop Buttons

This isn't clear from the figure, but the Start/Stop buttons would be color coded: green for Start and red for Stop. This gives clear, redundant cues that you set the time, and then press the green Start button to start the microwave. These buttons are also unambiguously labeled. Notice no double labeling exists, as it did in the original design, to confuse the issue.

Notice how incredibly simple it was to reach this design. You could even say it's fairly obvious, but that's the whole point. By picking a Scenario and designing only for that Scenario, the design task, too, is simplified. The result is both clear and easy to use.

Also notice that I didn't try adding a full numeric panel to input exact times such as 1:23. I've kept the original design's three-button approach to give Fred only rough time setting. This too is consistent with our basic Persona. Fred isn't going to cook his pizza for 5 minutes 38 seconds; he'll just set it for 5 or 6 minutes. When I've given this exercise out to others, they often add a numeric keypad. While this gives Fred precision, it also gives him many more buttons to cope with. Our Persona grounds that tendency by forcing us to ask what he is cooking and how. That precision adds too much complexity for the current tasks we're asking of Fred.

STAGE 2

Stage 1 was the first step. We now have to layer in the other task without compromising this design. For Fred to complete the second Scenario, thawing a bagel, he'll need some type of power setting. The previous design had a single Power button, which you had to press repeatedly to cycle through the 100 percent, 70 percent, 50 percent, 30 percent, and 10 percent power levels. Once the oven started, you had no indication of what power setting you were using because the display only showed the time remaining. In addition, there was the terrible gaff of only allowing you to change the power level at the beginning, just after you set the time.

We already have the design from Stage 1. All we want to do now is to add the power-level setting without causing too much disruption. But adding a power level as a percentage of the maximum setting is still a technical way to phrase this. What does this mean to Fred? It seems likely he'll be cooking on full power most of the time. So why does he have so many levels to choose from? Our given Scenarios make it clear Fred only needs two: High and Low. Common sense might indicate that we must have more power levels, but we're following the Scenarios at face value for the moment. Only put in what the Scenarios call for. Listening to the Scenarios first forces a certain clarity, which, even if slightly naïve, is worth seeing through to the end. This suggests the next stage in the design, as shown in Figure 6-3.

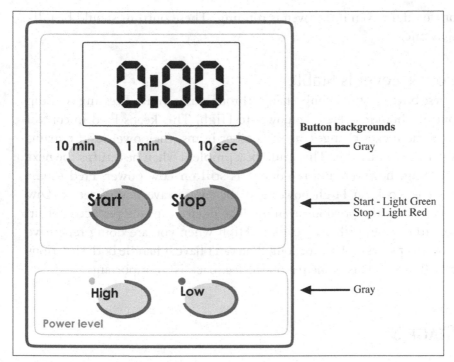

FIGURE 6-3. Stage 2 design.

Labeled Second Group Below to Set the Power

The original buttons formed a core group that were effective for basic tasks. I've enclosed them in a light gray line, so their self-contained nature is reinforced. The new High and Low buttons are also enclosed and labeled to make their functions clear. By placing these buttons just below the first group, they're clearly seen as an optional setting.

LEDs to Indicate Current Setting

Fred needs feedback, so he can be sure he's cooking at the right power. Pushing one of the power buttons lights up the LED next to the button, clearly showing which power level is in use.

Power Level Can Change at Any Time

To fix one of the Task-layer problems in the original design, these Power buttons should always respond — no matter if the door is open or closed, or even if the oven is running. These buttons should be fully dynamic.

Power Level Is Stable

These buttons should only change through user input. Pressing the Stop button shouldn't reset the power to High. This keeps Fred in control so, as he makes changes or cooks other items, the power level remains where he last used it. This could be a problem when he returns the next morning, however, and the device is still on Low power. Fred might want to cook on High power and the microwave is still set on Low power from the previous evening. The device can't be perfectly set up for either case. Either it resets to High when you are doing repetitive work or it stays on Low too long. You can't have it handle both situations equally well. This is the reason the feedback is so important.

STAGE 3

The Stage 2 design meets the first two Scenario needs. This is a good basic design that, given the cost constraints, is simple. And it's a far cry from the original product we saw at the beginning of the Design Break.

We aren't done yet, though. We've only completed the core tasks, but so far I've ignored the power user features that caused so much of the problem in the original design: the SuperCook buttons.

The SuperCook feature of this oven is difficult to use. It doesn't seem risky to say that most consumers would have a hard time getting all the settings correct. As a marketing device, its prime use is to look good enough in the store to differentiate the product. As with the previous power-setting simplification, the SuperCook choices need to be simplified and made accessible. If possible, it would also help if they add value to the user of the oven, instead of just adding a marketing-driven concept of feature differentiation.

You could easily make a point that these SuperCook features aren't required. The Stage 2 solution is more than 99 percent of what the population would need. Consumer products have many pressures, however, and one of them is to differentiate. To ship only the Stage 2 solution would most likely be more than most consumers need but, on the showroom floor, it probably isn't the model they'll choose. From a purely marketing perspective, there must be something special about the unit. Lots of variables other than the Stage 2 design, would factor into this, such as capacity, price, and styling. But most companies want something unique to show their device does something different than the other competing microwaves. This is clearly the motivation for the original and, unfortunately, ill-conceived SuperCook design. You can just hear the salesman saying, "And this baby can do eight additional automatic cooking tasks!"

To proceed, a good understanding must exist of what the user needs in the kitchen, and then offer it to them, so its value is apparent. This isn't something I can make up on the spot. Some consumer research must be done to help inform this decision. A focus group/user study I alluded to in the Persona insight would go a long way in understanding what normal people would use and value.

The key goal is to find three, not eight tasks that can have a strong value. Reducing their number, like reducing the power levels, makes it much easier to present, and then use these new features. By making the new features easier to use, they also become easier to explain, so they can be more effective as a differentiating factor on the showroom floor. Figure 6-4 shows how the Stage 3 design could look.

Simplified Functionality

Instead of a bewildering array of eight choices, restructure the buttons to only three. The choices I'm making are, admittedly, a bit arbitrary. My actual choices in this redesign aren't important; choosing only three is the critical issue. For example, the Popcorn button is something I've stolen from existing microwave designs, whose sole purpose is to cook microwave popcorn bags. They all happen to be the same weight and size, so the task flow is simple: put in the bag, close the door, and then push the Popcorn button.

The button for Potatoes is similar in that it's programmed to cook a single potato. Pushing it multiple times counts up on the display, so you can cook one, two, or more potatoes at a time.

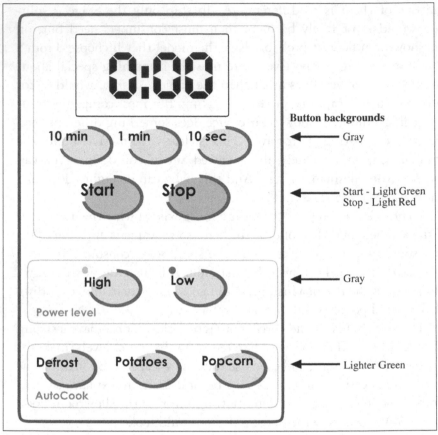

FIGURE 6-4. **Stage 3 design.**

I choose Defrost because it was a SuperCook option that was quite difficult to use because it involved choosing the meat type, as well as the weight. This was several button presses with little feedback, so making a mistake and ruining the meat would be easy. This version is intentionally much simpler. Press in the time, and then press Defrost. The customer is in control. Defrost something for five minutes and, if that isn't long enough, try again for another three minutes. While this isn't a complete feature as the original was attempting to be, it's so straightforward, it'll not only be discovered, it'll also be used. How this Defrost program works is much more transparent to the customer. Setting the time for too long is taking a risk. When in doubt, use a shorter time. As discovered with the first two Scenarios, many tasks are repetitive so, over time, the customers will become good at setting the time correctly. They will gain mastery over the product because it's the tool that puts them in control.

Another Group

Much like the power level, this next set of buttons – I've called the SuperCook here – is grouped and labeled, so it's clear these are extra features you don't have to use initially.

Green Coding to Mimic the Start Button

By coloring these buttons green, they become cousins to the Start button, so it's clear that pushing them turns on the oven.

COSTS

Saving Money

The new design is much simpler in software programming because so many fewer interaction details exist. The software costs of this new design will be lower, reflected not only in building costs, but also in software testing and user manual production. Some cost savings come from using a completely standard digital display instead of the custom display in the original design. I didn't go into much detail about this, but six special symbols were around the edge of the LCD display to help give some feedback to the AutoCook process.

Losing Money

The new design does use more buttons than the original, but these are inexpensive to add. There's additional cost to the LEDs next to the Power buttons but, again, that type of cost shouldn't cause great hardship. Given the savings in the LCD display, and the simplified software and hardware, assuming this new design will cost no more than the original seems reasonable.

WRAP UP

This design hasn't been user tested. I'm sure a quick user study would help iron out a few problems, most likely with labeling but, of course, many other things might pop up. I would also pay close attention to the LED feedback on the power level buttons. They might not be effective and could need to be more aggressive in getting the user's attention, such as blinking or being brighter. But, given these caveats, I have no doubt this unit, for the same price as the original, would do much better in most homes.

You could argue that my version of SuperCook isn't fancy enough and you'd need to roll in even more features to distinguish the oven. This might be so, but this unit isn't meant to be a high-end microwave – only a better version than the one we started with, without raising the component costs. Even though I only have three features and the original has eight, this doesn't make a significant marketing difference. Not only is it discoverable and usable, but it still exists as a marketing concept that can be hyped on the box for differentiation.

This design followed a simple Persona/Scenario model. This Design Break isn't about creating the ultimate low-end microwave but, instead, it's about showing how to follow a simple, but effective, tool through to a design. Most likely, more work on the Scenarios would expose further design considerations. For example, a need might exist for a third power-level setting, so you would have High, Medium, and Low. Upcoming chapters discuss going beyond the obvious functions and attempting to make more innovative products.

The key point of this exercise is this: once you focus on a Persona and its core Scenario, the design tends to suggest itself. By simplifying your requirements, you almost automatically simplify your design. It practically designs itself.

Feature Blindness

Simple things should be simple and complex things should be possible.

—*Alan Kay*

INTRODUCTION

In the previous chapters, I showed how curing user blindness improves the early stages of the product process. It gives you a more precise concept of the target users and a stronger understanding of what is important to them. Personas and Scenarios are effective tools at working from the bottom up, uncovering the core tasks the product must satisfy for the user.

Feature blindness is the next blindness we must cure. *Feature blindness* comes from being blinded by the *feature list*, a checklist of must-have, whizzy new technology to be included in the product. It's all too easy to see a product only as a list of features. If the list is small, the product appears not to be competitive. Project teams are blinded by features because they tend to focus only on cramming as many into the product as possible.

Feature lists tend to work from the top down, bestowing requirements that must be in the product. This isn't something to get upset about — it's simply a fact of life. The world of business is a complicated place and valid reasons exist for these types of requirements. These top-down feature pressures tend to conflict with the bottom-up discoveries that made the Persona and Scenario work, however. Persona and Scenario work focuses the product concept to meet the basic needs of the target user. Feature lists, on the other hand, complicate the design by turning the product into a smorgasbord of options. The poor user stares at a busy display stuffed with icons, menus, and buttons, and doesn't know where to start. In effect, the user doesn't know what to ignore. Becoming proficient with these types of products is a complicated learning curve of understanding what to filter out to do the small subset of functionality necessary.

To achieve Simplicity, you have to tame the feature list and not let it push you around. I will relent to a certain amount of outside pressure that brings in required features. All professionals must be able to work with these situations, but this must be done in a disciplined manner, so you control the feature list, not the other way around. A tiny subset of the feature list is usually used with any frequency – the classic 80/20 split applies here as well – where 80 percent of the users will use only 20 percent of the product. In many cases, this is closer to a 90/10 split.

You might think my solution to this tension is to remove most features from a product. While this would help create Simplicity, it's unnecessarily harsh and it wouldn't have the depth required for repeated or more experienced use. This solution wouldn't grow into a user's needs as they transition from initial to accomplished use. The solution is more subtle: uncover and prioritize the features, and discover a core set that must be simple and extremely approachable. This will be the essence of the product everyone will use. Design first for this core set, and then layer on the additional functions, so they're in the product, but not at the expense of the core design.

The previous Design Break gave a few hints as to how to do this. In this chapter, I present three Insights that discuss how to do it in more detail. Insight 3 – unFeatures – is about the types of features usually found by designers, but never included in marketing feature lists. This is necessary to make sure the feature list isn't only a marketing-inspired laundry list, but a more thorough list of what the complete product will require. Insight 4, "The Priority Trick," is a simple tool to take a seemingly endless list of features and give it some direction, so you know what to design first. Insight 5, "Make the Easy, Easy and the Hard,

Hard" is a technique for creating a simple design first, and then layering on the addition high-end features.

INSIGHT 3 – UNFEATURES: THERE'S MORE THAN MEETS THE EYE

The first step in curing feature blindness is to think outside the box. Most companies only think in terms of big features, such as adding Bluetooth to the PDA or GPRS to the phone. But when you're designing a consumer product, you're not only designing features, you're also designing a product that fits into someone's life. You have to start thinking through the consumer's eyes.

Big features are important in planning a product but, often, many little features end up causing several problems later on in the product cycle. Because most of the focus is on the big features, these little problems usually aren't discovered until late in the product cycle. At this point, however, the product is too far along and these problems get turned into feature requests for the next release.

A common example would be getting the product configured and set up when the user first gets the product out of the box, such as the Bluetooth headset and the mobile phone. In focusing on the big feature – Bluetooth – this configuration problem is pushed off until it's far too late in the product cycle to resolve it.

This has happened often enough that I call these things *unFeatures*, which are common things that go wrong with the product and, which, initially, are never put on to a feature list. These problems are handled, usually badly, at the end of a product when the first working prototypes start making these issues glaring and no longer capable of being ignored.

What's frustrating is if you take an aggressive approach to these problems early in the design process, you can solve many of them fairly cheaply and easily. The trick is to start this process early, when you have time in the schedule to fix them simply and painlessly.

UnFeatures is a broad set of problems that needs to grow over time. The following is a list of the major unFeatures that seem to crop up in most products I've worked on. This list isn't exhaustive. It's simply representative of many problems I've found in the past.

Warning: the following concepts have been known to cause drowsiness in product managers.

Product Setup

What does it take to get your product out of the box and working? As in my nirvana Scenario for Bluetooth in the introduction, can you simply break open the box and start using the product? If not, what are the steps to setting it up? What information is needed to complete the setup?

VCR Example

Most modern VCRs have the capability to search for available stations automatically. You usually have to dig around a bit to discover it, finding the Menu button on the remote, going to the configuration screen, selecting channel set up, and then choosing something usually called Autoscan.

My latest VCR offered to do this automatically when I first turned it on. Was this lots of extra work? No. The feature had already been implemented for years and it was a fairly small effort to detect the right conditions where the power was turned on and to offer it to the user automatically.

Innovator and early adopter types of users can often cope with product setup problems because they read the manual and spend the time going through the entire setup process. The more a product tries to capture a mass market, however, the more it has to make setup as easy as possible.

Reliability and Error Recovery

This sounds so boring, but it's one of the most infuriating aspects of using consumer electronics. Many times, a situation occurs when handling an error is difficult and few options exist to the programmer. In these situations, the user is usually forced to deal with the problem, in a completely baffling way.

The example I'd use here would be the GPRS study discussed earlier. Most new fancy technology is laden with reliability problems, so when we did our initial Scenarios, we actively looked for this. While we didn't find all the possible errors, we were able to find some nasty ones. This type of information is extremely valuable in planning product strategy.

A common, but misguided belief exists that when an error occurs, it must be reported to the user at once. This is the high-tech equivalent of crying wolf. Errors pop up frequently and, often, the users don't have the information they need or the ability to solve the problem easily. Microprocessors have enough computing power that we should expect companies to try a little harder to solve problems for the user, instead of simply throwing them up for the user to see. An example here would be a desktop computer program that can't find a specific file. If it can't be found, the common solution is to show a Can't find it error message. Slightly better is to offer a Look around button, which makes the user paw through the hundreds of folders on the hard disk. Why not offer an Automatically Search button that makes the computer do all the work? It might take a whopping 30 seconds, but it would be much faster than making the user do it.

Another example comes from mobile phones. A common problem is getting a network error when you send a text message. For whatever reason, the message didn't go through. The classic approach to this error is to inform the user. The user must then try again to send the message. A much more useful approach would be to offer to resend the message automatically in a few minutes.

This isn't simply about making the user's life a little easier. It's about avoiding situations that can cause trouble and affect product acceptance. Errors are usually product opportunities waiting to happen.

Repetitive or Discontinuous Task Flow

What does it take to use the product for common, usually repetitive, tasks? It is all too easy to mark a feature as functionally complete, but using it can be irritating. A classic example here would be deleting an e-mail from an inbox. In one product I was working on, you had to open the e-mail first, choose the menu item Delete, and then answer an "Are you the user?" alert. The Delete Mail feature was certainly in the product but this multi-step process drove users crazy because one of the most frequent tasks with this product was to delete potentially dozens of e-mails a day!

I was on a project with this exact problem. As we went into the product design with this task-flow problem in mind, I discussed with the programmers the capability to have a deleted folder, so items could be deleted but, if necessary, undeleted from this folder later. Because it was early in the project, this was an easy thing for them to add. We also made it possible to delete an item directly from the list view, so you could delete three e-mails with only three button pushes. This was well received and a significant improvement to the product. It wasn't hard to add, but it would never have been added if we'd discussed it late in the beta testing phase.

Other task-flow problems come not from repetition, but from placement. For example, many PDA-type devices have a mishmash of setting controls to configure e-mail, making the user go to a modem control panel, a networking control panel, a phone control panel, and more. Not only is the flow complex, but it also involves considerable navigation expertise to know where to go to find all these nuggets of functionality.

Many solutions exist to this type of problem – from a wizard that papers over the underlying confusion or a more ambitious rewrite of the control panels to reorganize them. The point here is you need to use Scenarios to go through a few core tasks to uncover what it will be like to use the product and make sure the user isn't hopping all over the place to use it.

Sense of Place

Sense of place refers to the users having a good understanding of where they are and, more importantly, where they can go. Too many products have a weak navigation model, so users don't understand where they are. In the next Design Break, we'll study an MP3 player that had this problem. Its navigational model was primarily through a large number of buttons on the face of the product. These buttons did enable the user to navigate, but they were poor at feedback. It wasn't clear where you were in the product by looking at the screen, which made for a confusing and frustrating product.

A sense of place is not only about simple and consistent navigation, it's about good, even redundant feedback, so the users have a strong understanding of where they are. In one mobile phone product I was working on, each application ended up looking much the same containing a list of text items: an e-mail list, a contact list, and meeting list, and so on. I placed a small icon in front of each item. This wasted valuable screen space, but it was instrumental in helping the user differentiate each list. In user testing, subjects were able to tell at a glance where they were and were better able to know what they wanted to do next.

How to Do It

Management must know that unFeatures exist and ask that they're included in the product discussions. Designers must use unFeatures to motivate Persona/Scenario work to discover problems. In both cases, both sides now have a way of discussing these unknown problems and, more importantly, attacking them earlier in the product cycle.

Handling unFeatures is nothing more than a variation of the earlier Persona/Scenario work. The small difference is that management needs to understand these unFeatures almost always occur and need to be addressed as part of the product strategy.

Things That Go Wrong

The biggest problem is that unFeatures are considered too soft and not worth pursuing until later in the project. The best way to overcome this concern is by showing how simple it is to address the unFeatures problem. It doesn't take long to run a few Persona/Scenarios through the previously listed unFeatures in an exploratory way to create a list of concerns. This type of report will always be welcomed because it's a list of potential threats to the product success.

The challenge in doing unFeature work is you can easily find some fairly obvious problems that aren't going to be fixed any time soon because of costs, infrastructure limitations, or even bad battery life. UnFeatures work can easily find issues to fix that are clearly beyond the scope of the project. The problems that are found that can be addressed, however, easily make this a valuable exercise.

Insight 4 – The Priority Trick

What It Is

Even though we've established that the feature list needs to be tamed and prioritized, unFeatures usually add more to the main feature list as you discover new, previously unknown issues that need addressing. This feels like a step backward because the list is now growing! The feature list often feels like the enemy because it embodies the unrealistic forces that are cramming too much into the product in the first place and, yet, here we are adding to this list. We're adding things that have a high priority, however. Our items are well motivated and can be shown to have strong impact on the overall quality of the product. The Priority Trick is a simple tool to tame this growing list, wrestling it into an order that enables you to discuss and solve the problems in a way that informs the design, not complicates it.

Why It's Important

A long feature list isn't inherently bad. The problem is in trying to design for all its features at once. This pollutes the design by forcing the product to show too many details to the user at once, mixing the high-volume simple functions along with the low-volume complex functions. By prioritizing the features based on your Persona/Scenario work, you'll have a way of approaching the list in a calmer way, so your design can handle the important features first.

How to Do It

This Insight is rather straightforward to explain. It might, however, create quite an entertaining meeting. Create a numbered list of all the critical features being asked of the project. Be sure to include the ones that come from the unFeatures work. Have each member of the product team then rank each feature two ways. The first way is for the member to list his or her understanding of how frequently the feature will be used: rarely (1), moderately (2), or frequently (3). The next way is to rank the same list by importance to the product: low (1), useful (2), or critical (3). All these rankings must be done from the perspective of the Personas you created, though, not from your own personal position. This is crucial because it separates personal beliefs from the needs of the target consumer.

For example, let's take two features of a consumer-focused e-mail program that works through the television. We'll use Earl, a retired steelworker as our Persona. Reading a newly arrived e-mail is a feature that seems like it would be frequently used and of critical value to Earl. Adding the capability to create Filters, which lets Earl automatically route e-mails into folders would rarely be used because he wouldn't receive that much e-mail. That feature would probably also score a low priority for the product.

A common pressure in this type of voting is that a large number of items are ranked both frequent and critical. To force a more structured voting pattern, require each person to have his or her votes evenly distributed. So, if twelve items are in the list, you can have no more that four of each type. This makes some people uncomfortable because they worry about having too many low votes. The point here isn't to remove everything, but to prioritize everything. It doesn't do any good to make everything a 1/1 vote.

The votes are collected and the two rankings are added together for each feature. The list is then sorted with the features with the highest numbers at the top. This exercise isn't as numerically perfect as it might first sound. The purpose is to get the input and buy-in of the product team. By doing this vote as a group activity, you'll undoubtedly force some strong discussion. Some will vote without regard to the Persona. Others will vote only for their favorite feature. This should be expected. By getting these little differences out in the open, you can discuss the types of forces that can derail a product as it moves through production.

Once the voting has become stable, you have one more decision to make. The team must draw a line to separate the top critical features of the product. The voting will cluster a bit, so this is usually fairly easy. As a general rule of thumb, this subset should be no more than a third of the original list. This is our final goal: a prioritized list that shows you what must go into the product and, therefore, must be reflected in the design. This prioritization is a powerful tool because it eliminates the confusion that comes from a checklist of features.

In addition, those items at the bottom of the priority list should be carefully questioned. They needn't be removed. Revisiting them is certainly worthwhile. Removing an item now is much better than removing it later because this saves considerable time down the road.

What Goes Wrong

The biggest problem with this Insight is working with an unfriendly feature list. If you're not careful, vague technology items will be on it like "Support 802.11," a required industry standard you simply must have for this product. Before you continue, try breaking this up through Scenarios and unFeatures into subtasks that make more sense from a user's perspective. Vague technology items create trouble.

Another problem is the initial list can occasionally be quite long. Once it gets up to more than 20, the voting starts to get cumbersome. What usually helps in this situation is to focus on substantial features, not small corners. This isn't as arbitrary as it might sound. A fairly common-sense approach can remove such things as bug fixes and small additions to existing features.

Insight 5 – Make the Easy, Easy and the Hard, Hard

What It Is

Once you prioritized the feature list, you're in a strong position to design the core of the product. With this design in place, you can then add the more advanced features on top.

The previous Design Break about the microwave oven was a simple example, but it showed how having a reduced set of features tends to clarify the design and allows it to form much more easily, sometimes almost effortlessly. This Insight discusses layering in the remainder of the prioritized features without compromising this simple core design.

The core design is important. You have 90 percent of the battle won because the design handles the vast majority of the user's key tasks. This gives you two strong advantages. The first is the remaining complex functions are usually done by more sophisticated users. They can cope better with a more complex design. The second point is a hard one for design purists to accept, but it's simply that it doesn't matter as much if you get the design for these more complex features wrong. This doesn't mean you should ever make a secondary feature horrible. Instead, it means the further you get from the primary feature, the less pressure exists to get it perfect – a moderate solution will do just fine.

The essence of this Insight is to put the remaining features in, but to put them in so they don't compromise the Simplicity you've already achieved.

How to Do It: Showing too Much Detail with a Single Feature

It's all too easy to give a feature too many "knobs," which allows the user to set too many options. Why settle for only a Low, Medium, and High choice when you can offer a type-in field that enables users to set the field with anything between 1 and 100? Clearly, the proper answer depends on the situation, but this standard engineering approach is to offer as much flexibility as possible. I would claim they don't understand how the device will be used, so they're in doubt about what's important. This means they pile on the flexibility just to be safe.

As an example, let's go back to the microwave redesign in the previous Design Break. The original design had the capability to set five different levels of power. This flexibility created complexity as the single Power button now had to cycle through all five power states. The first press got you 100 percent power, the next 70 percent, the next 50 percent, and so forth. If you went too far, you had to press it five more times to cycle around to the correct state. This type of cycling button always causes problems because it not only hides a function, but it also makes it hard to use and provides little feedback. It wasn't at all clear in our Scenario work that the user needed much more than Low and High settings. The need to have the power that flexible wasn't justified.

My redesign of the Power button removed some of the flexibility by only offering two or three levels of power. This allows three top-level buttons with an LED for feedback. By reducing the depth of a feature slightly, the usability increased greatly.

Some of you might say this appears to contradict my $1 + 1 = 3$ rule because I'm adding more buttons, instead of removing them. Well, high marks for paying attention. I agree we're adding more buttons so we're increasing the number of choices. What counterbalances the extra buttons is the Power feature is now labeled as a group of buttons and is now much more visible and easier for the user to parse. Originally, the Power button was buried in a sea of identical buttons, creating parsing shock and making it far too hard to find. By grouping the Power buttons, I made the feature much more obvious. Of course, I also removed many of the other extraneous buttons, which helped bring out the obvious use of the Power button group.

Another example was at Apple Computer, where I was brought a Print dialog box for a new dot-matrix printer. All sorts of options were onscreen, offering bidirectional printing, bit thinning, and others, which the user had to choose before pressing the Print button. In all, there were 28 possible combinations. At the time, Apple had a simple print model that usually gave the user three choices for print quality:

Draft, Better, and Best. For most people, these choices were more than enough for the type of output they wanted. By mapping the bidirectional and bit-thinning options to the right user goal of Draft, Better, and Best, the user had the benefit of the choices, without the parsing shock of having to understand which was required and when. Too much flexibility often hides a misperception of what the user needs. If you see the work through technocolored glasses, everything needs to be set. On the other hand, if you see the world through Persona colored glasses, you realize that 99 percent of the time, users want to do two or three things and you create your design around those tasks, not the technology.

How to Do It: Get It out of the Way

This is a fairly straightforward trick. When you have an advanced feature you need to layer into your core design, don't put it in at the top level. You should effectively bury the feature in a menu item or some other layered interface level, such as a control panel. The advanced user will be able to find it and this keeps the parsing load low for the introductory user. This often causes a problem because super-cool features are buried away, which bothers some people. If you've done your homework properly, however, these buried tasks aren't high on the priority list, so making the user dig shouldn't be a problem. People who can't abide this hiding clearly don't agree it should be lowered in priority. You must address this issue by either convincing these people of the priority or by raising it and changing the core design.

A classic example here would be a PDA I designed for Symbian, which had the capability to change the font size for each application. Many programmers wanted up-front icon buttons in the view to let you choose between small, medium, and large fonts. This was primarily used by power users to switch to a smaller font to force more information in the display. Adding these buttons to every view would certainly make this feature easier to see and faster for the programmers, but it also clearly increased the parsing shock. I made sure the default font was clear and legible, so for the initial use out of the box, the display was highly legible. My goal, and my first priority, was to reduce the need to *increase* the font of poorly sighted users. Next was to worry about the yahoos who wanted to cram as much text on the screen as possible. For them, I had a Font size menu item that brought up a dialog box to set the font to three sizes. Once set, the font was remembered, so they didn't have to go back to reset it.

Some argued this was clunky because power users needed to go through each application and rummage through the menus. It was "lots of extra work" for them. Absolutely! I can't think of a better trade-off because no group can cope more with this type of solution and, more importantly, this type of font change usually happens only once, and then it's stable for a long time, so the "cost" isn't repeated often. The benefit was a significantly cleaner, calmer screen. The parsing shock was reduced, which also enhanced the sense of place.

How to Do It: Make the User Click More

This is a slight variation on the previous rule. I'm putting it into this form because I get it as a frequent complaint: "But that means it will be an extra two clicks to do this!" Damn straight. The feature that's now two clicks away wasn't at the top of the priority list, so it doesn't deserve a top-level placement, especially because doing so would have a negative impact on those features that are much higher on the list.

Chapter 2 I discussed a mobile phone manufacturer that replaced a Delete button with three New buttons. One justification we were told was that burying the new Fax option under a menu was "too many taps away" and not an acceptable solution. We agreed it was further away, but we didn't think making Delete even more clicks than Fax was consistent with our prioritized feature list.

This type of layering is hard work and usually provokes heated debate. This is why I stress that everyone in the product cycle should share in these concepts, so you can raise your vocabulary and make decisions everyone can understand.

This is why I'm setting out in such detail the concepts of Personas, Scenarios, and Prioritized feature lists. These are tools that increase your communication vocabulary. Now you can say things like "This change has a major impact on our third core task, which you agreed to last month. We must find a way to keep this core task in place."

How to Do It: Reduce Complex Questions to the User

Another form of parsing shock comes from an error dialog box offering an exhaustive list of options. The vast majority of the time, the user would only need to make a few simple choices but, occasionally, things get so mucked up, developers give users too many options to get out of a messy situation. This confuses the users because they're given choices for aspects of the problem that are subtle and beyond their immediate grasp. What often happens is what I call the moth-to-the-flame syndrome, where users are confused about what to do so, to be safe, they turn on everything they can to make sure they're covered. This is exactly what the original programmers didn't want to happen and this can cause more problems than it creates.

A perfect example of this is when Personal File Sharing was added to the Macintosh back in System 7, when there was a need for the user to set folder privileges. Clearly not a task you want most consumers to deal with. To its credit, there was a rather nice design that let you pick what you wanted to share and then select from a simplified menu of sharing choices. This all worked quite well. The problem came with a little check box at the bottom of the dialog box: Copy privileges to all enclosed folders.

The need for the check box was obscure. Most people were either sharing a single folder or an entire drive. With the case of a single folder, this choice made no sense. With an entire drive, you didn't want to do this because it would take a long time to run through and change all the folders. Why even have this option at all? Good question. The motivation was to clean up a drive's subfolders that had mixed folder settings back into a pristine state: a recovery situation for a high-end situation gone wrong.

This feature clearly wasn't needed the vast majority of the time. What made this particular check box so bad was that novice users exhibited the moth-to-the-flame syndrome, interpreting it incorrectly, thinking if they didn't check it, stuff inside wouldn't get shared, so they would check it and, sometimes, have to wait minutes while useless folder thrashing took place.

The solution is to layer this in some way. Eliminate the check box entirely and have the Save button. If the object in question was a single folder, no problem: set the single folder and you're done. If there were subfolders, then do a quick test, reading if a mixture of preferences existed, and then offer a choice *at that point* with some explanatory text.

The programmers were worried this type of checking would slow things down, running through dozens, if not hundreds, of folders needlessly. This was a good valid concern, but of no real consequence. The first is that checking this many folders really didn't take but a few seconds the vast majority of the time and the second was that this activity of setting the folder privileges was a very low volume task so even if it did take a whopping 15 seconds, it wouldn't be done that often.

This is a great example of the type of work it takes to Make the Easy, Easy and the Hard, Hard. Making it "easy" brings up lots of issues that make the product team nervous as a "simple solution" does open up some end cases that may not be handled cleanly. There is always a tradeoff that needs to be made balancing the potential for a feature to be used incorrectly and one which makes is slightly slower to use.

Why It's Important

Designing like this; making higher-end functions slightly harder to use, often creates intense arguments from programmers who feel this "dumbs down" the product. This appears only to punish those users who take the time to understand technology and try to use it to its fullest potential. This isn't about punishing power users, but rather *not* punishing the initial users. Making the initial design solution elegant and simple has benefits for all users. This isn't only about placing higher-end features on the top shelf, but making sure all the frequent and critical features are on the low shelf. This can not only help the user learn the device, but it can also help the user use the device in a more proficient way because the simpler design will also be streamlined and faster, even for the power users.

Things That Go Wrong

Getting a design based around the high-priority tasks is rarely the problem. As I stated earlier, it almost designs itself. The real difficulty comes in layering on the additional functions because they can easily make deep changes to the initial design. This is the primary reason I have Design Breaks in this book: to give examples of how this works. While most things can be placed into a menu or into a dialog box, at times, a change to the core design can't be avoided. No master rules exist to make this process easy for you. This, in general, comes from experience. I call out this problem in the following Design Break, so you have one example of how such a trade-off is made.

The other problem tends to be political. Placing things out of the way seems so counterproductive, many people have a hard time accepting it. Two forces are here. The first is the core tasks must be preserved and value must be attached to this. Otherwise, these types of tradeoffs will never be accepted. The other force is the real concern that its possible to place a feature a little too far away. This Insight isn't license to bury everything under three levels of hierarchical menus. This isn't usually much of a problem because a simple design that handles the core tasks usually has a secondary spot to park most of the advanced features.

CONCLUSION

As with user blindness, this process must be shared at some level with the product team. It doesn't do any good to tame the feature list and be over-ridden by management. Features are easy to list and overuse as a management and planning tool. We have to start treating the feature list as a source of design confusion. The three Insights in this chapter can help the team interact with the feature list in a disciplined manner, so the design, not the feature list, is in control. UnFeatures make sure the feature list is complete and isn't missing some obvious bits that will significantly affect the viability of the product. The Priority Trick drives a team activity that will prioritize the adjusted feature list to make sure the core features are tackled and designed first. Once you have a design that meets only these needs, then make the hard, hard and build a layered design, one that adds the advanced tasks with care, making sure the core design isn't compromised.

Notice this chapter doesn't talk much about creating this core design. Too many domains exist with individual rules and tradeoffs to make such a chapter generic. The focus here is on creating a shared team approach that management, marketing, development, and design can all use to create an environment where product decisions can be made to support the product and set it up to succeed.

As I said before, most bad products are bad before the designers ever get involved. They are poorly motivated, with a confusing set of priorities and an inability to think clearly about what the product needs to do. The insights in this chapter are a step in correcting these problems.

Design Break: MP3 Player

8

Understanding human needs is half the job of meeting them.

—*Adlai Stevenson*

This Design Break is definitely more substantial than the previous two. The point here is to use the previous insights to give you an idea of how they can be used. Much like the microwave oven, I'll take an existing product and create a new design that improves it, while not significantly increasing the cost of the device. I'll go a little further, though, and discuss more innovative ideas that come from the Scenario work.

PROBLEM

This is a redesign of a popular MP3 player that hit the market in 2001. The most distinguishing feature of this MP3 player was the use of a small hard disk instead of RAM for music storage, so you could contain over 100 CDs worth of music on the device. This was a huge leap forward from other players, which had difficulty holding even two hours of music.

The leap didn't stop there, however. This MP3 player had the capability to record with an external microphone. It also enabled you to create playlists and even use special digital processing to change the effects of the playback simulating concert hall or jazz club acoustics.

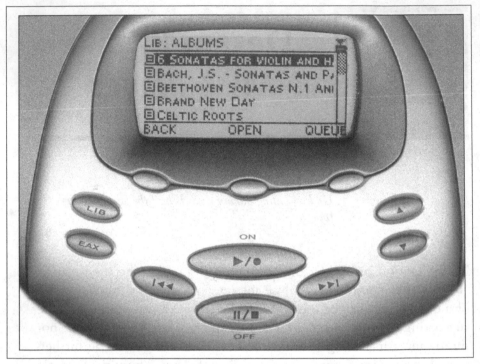

FIGURE 8-1. Original MP3 design.

The MP3 player, as shown in Figure 8-1, was also rather hard to use. Not to the early adopters, though, because they tend to overlook design problems in order to get significant new capabilities. While this was clearly an early adopter design, this MP3 player did sell fairly well into this emerging market because its capacity was so much higher that previous players. This product would be hard pressed to make it into the mainstream consumer market, though, as it's currently designed. The usability problems would be a turn-off to more laggard-type users and another, more streamlined competitor, would most likely steal its thunder. This is a good machine for us to redesign because it can show a transition from early adopter to a more mainstream user frame of design.

ANALYSIS

Hardware

This machine has a fairly generous screen – roughly 128 pixels wide by 64 pixels tall – for a consumer electronic device. It has 11 buttons on the front, a surprisingly large number. The three buttons at the top are what are called *soft buttons*, which are buttons whose function changes, depending on context. In the previous figure, you can see how the left soft button is labeled Back. The difficulty with soft buttons is they're a means to creating even more buttons. Eleven is already an overwhelming number for a device like this. Having three of these buttons change, effectively adding even more virtual buttons to the mix, makes for a challenging design to understand and use easily.

Of course, soft buttons can be used well, but they're so easily used incorrectly. You've seen this before in the microwave example where the Power-level setting was hidden under a single button, so you had to watch the screen to see at which level you were located and how many more presses you needed to reach your goal. As a general rule, I try hard to avoid soft buttons because they tend to create, rather than solve, complexity. Of course, getting rid of soft buttons isn't only a Presentation layer problem. You have to change the Task layer significantly to get around the initial design philosophy.

Screen Design

The look on the screen is rather retro PC because it has a scroll bar on the screen. This is an example of *default thinking*, which I discuss later in Insight 6. The designers probably assumed most personal computers have scroll bars, so adding them here was an acceptable practice. Why this decision is so suspect is because the design of this particular scroll bar is but a pale shadow of the original desktop version: it's for information display only. Using a mouse or a pen to tap on the scroll bar, as you would on a computer, isn't possible.

For consumer devices such as this, scroll bars might an option, but they should be used only as a last resort. I think most screens for a device like this should be designed never to scroll, completely eliminating the need for the scroll bars. For cases when the screen needs to scroll through a long list of songs, it will be an alphabetized list, which naturally lets you know where you are in the list without the complication of a scroll bar. If this analysis seems a bit radical to you, look at almost any mobile phone. It doesn't use a scroll bar when running through the list of contacts in the phone book, yet the interaction feels natural. What is obvious often depends on your initial perspective. Another point is this: to fit the soft button labels on the screen, the display font has been made quite small. A font of this low resolution will have strong consequences, not only for older users, but also for younger ones who want to use it in lower light situations.

Initial Goals

So, before we even discuss Personas, we have a few guiding principles to remember.

- Reduce button count to simplify learning
- Avoid soft buttons for the same reason
- Reduce PC clutter to simplify presentation
- Increase font size to increase legibility

Last Comments

To play music on this device, the consumer must understand the concept of "queuing" music versus playing music. For this device, music is placed first into a queue, and then played. This allows more flexibility because, while the device is playing one track, you can queue up another to be played next. To make things a bit easier, if you navigate down to an album and press Play, the device will queue and play the music, all at the same time. This all sounds vaguely reasonable until you discover that when you come back to play another album, when you press Play again, it queues your new request after the first album, and starts from the top, playing the first album over. To listen to only a second album, you must clear the queue and play the second album.

This clearly has benefits if your primary task is to create a long playing list of music from bits and pieces, letting you create a mix of music. This is, indeed, powerful, but it's worth discussing whether the power is worth the complexity.

PERSONA AND SCENARIOS

I'll create two personas here: Steve and Lisa. Neither one will be a geek power user, but both will be heavy music lovers who have some fairly specific needs.

Steve

Steve is 18 and is still in high school. He lives with his parents and drives a beat-up Subaru. Steve currently hauls around a pack of CDs and a CD Walkman wherever he goes. Because Steve's taste in music is well developed, his friends often want to know what he's currently listening to. Steve is going through an acoustic phase, collecting acoustic versions of his favorite groups from the Internet and burning his own custom CDs. When he's at home, Steve likes to play music, with his friends and while he's studying.

Lisa

Lisa is a professional cellist, who is age 32, single, and lives in an apartment. She doesn't own a car, and she takes the bus to and from work. Lisa has a fairly stable set of classic and modern music she listens to regularly, but she tends to listen at home. She also makes recordings of her practice sessions on cassette tape, but finds the whole thing a bit cumbersome and doesn't like the hassle of all those tapes. At home, Lisa has a nice stereo because when she listens to her music, she appreciates high-fidelity reproduction.

Scenario 1: First Get the Product

Both Personas are going to need to get this product out of a box and set it up the first time. A magical solution would be to have all their music appear on the device. Clearly, this is a bit of a stretch, but what could we do to get the songs transferred? Steve seems a little better placed because he's clearly a desktop PC user, so he might already have a large collection of digital music files. This isn't clear with Lisa. A big consideration is going to be getting her CD on to the device easily. If this takes hours, she probably won't bother. This points to a key strategic decision that needs to be made: does this product ignore novice computer users or does it make bridging over to this device possible for them? If bridging is the goal, a strong PC application will need to look up the track names, encode, and then download the songs to the unit.

Scenario 2: Going for a Walk

Assuming the unit has most of the base songs on the device, let's take it for a walk. It seems likely this will require headphones. Given that Steve and Lisa both will use this while they're in motion, it seems likely that volume will be an obvious thing to adjust. Many volume solutions are on the market today, with everything from controls in the headset itself to something on the device. Many options need to be discussed with the team. Having the control on the headset seems the most direct and sensible design. If it does have to be on the device, though, then it must be easy to reach because Steve and Lisa will both probably be rummaging around in a bag or a backpack when they're trying to set it. In this case, the volume control should be a stiff analog dial, large and easily visible on the unit. Having some means of knowing how far the dial is rotated would be helpful, so they should have some visual indication about how high the volume is set before you put on the headsets.

Scenario 3: Taking a Drive

Steve might want to listen to the music in his car. This suggests some way of either plugging it in to his car stereo or using an FM transmitter to play through the radio. These both have cost implications but, again, this needs to be discussed in a broader context because having a device work wirelessly in your car could have a big cool factor for some people.

One problem with the FM transmitter idea is it might be cumbersome to be fiddling with a small screen display while you're getting into a car, especially if it's cold and you're bundled up. This suggests a hardware switch you could switch from headphones to radio transmission. You could easily see this button being left on accidentally, though, so it might be useful to make the switch obvious in some way – either by making it large and colorful, where switching on FM exposes some red paint, or to have a blinking LED to make sure you know it's on. All of these possible features would need to be brainstormed with the development team to find the most cost-effective solution.

Scenario 4: Playing Music

Lisa seems the most likely to want to play her music like a traditional CD player, picking a CD and letting it run. Steve also would probably use the player this way, but he seems to like to share his musical finds with his friends, so Steve will most likely want to pick individual songs to play.

In sharing with friends, a problem exists because, as a headphone-only device, they would have to share the headphones one at a time. The FM transmitter idea from the previous Scenario is interesting because it means that anywhere Steve can find an FM radio, he can share his music. Bringing along a small set of speakers or a patch cord to plug into a friends stereo seems a bit complicated. All Steve wants to bring with him are the device and the headphones.

In fact, this triggers another idea: if the unit had FM headphones, Steve could have a cable-free experience using the device. This sounds a bit radical because many technical issues must be considered, such as battery life, sound quality, and so forth, but the idea could potentially be innovative.

Lisa would like to play her music at home. She already has a nice stereo and lots of CDs, so it isn't clear if this unit will rival her CD jukebox at home. If Lisa were to use this unit at home, the FM idea again presents itself, but we also have to look at standard solutions. If there were only an output jack on the device, it could be hooked up directly to Lisa's stereo. This is a bit cumbersome, though, because Lisa would have to switch her stereo to an alternative input source and leave the patch cord next to the machine, so she could plug it in more easily.

As for listening to music, purists out there like to have an equalizer or digital effects enhancer to make their music sound its best. I don't see the value of this in either of the current Personas. If this does become of value, however, it doesn't strike me as necessary that the full spectrum equalizer control is necessary when listening to music on the move. Most likely, a small number of presets, such as classical or concert hall, would be enough and, once either Persona picks one, they'll probably keep it that way. This implies that if this feature is in the product, it would be best left up to the PC to create these settingsand only let the device pick from a small set.

Scenario 5: Playing from a Long List

The primary innovation this product brings is the capability to play lots of music. What does it mean to play a CD on a device that can contain over 100 CDs? How can Lisa or Steve pick a song easily from this long list?

Clearly, you're going to need some browsing structure here. There's a natural hierarchy to exploit by grouping songs into CDs, and then into CDs by artist. It seems entirely likely there won't be much depth to this hierarchy, however, so scrolling through 100 CDs will require scrolling through potentially 30–40 artists. This will only get worse as the technology matures and even more music can be stored.

So, even before you lay down a single pixel, you know you'll need some decent response time/scrolling speed on this device. This would be a heavy discussion with the technical director to make sure you understand the screen refresh rates and the speed of the processor to drive the display. We can't do anything about that in this book, but this is an infrastructure layer detail of the design we'd have to nail down.

A second point would be to discuss the possibility of a scroll wheel on the device to move quickly through the list. If a fairly low-price part exists, a large marketing build up of this scroller could occur because it would clearly differentiate the product and make it more appealing.

Steve also points out that he collects Internet music, so he'll have music that will break out of the classic CD categorization. This isn't as critical as the basic "Play CD" approach, but it does lead into the playlist concept. *Playlists* appear to be a music power-user type of feature where you want to organize your music in a particular order – either to group a bunch of songs together as Steve does with acoustic tracks or as a long list for prolonged listening. Creating this type of long list is something the desktop PC appears significantly better suited to do, so while we can offload that task from the device, that still leaves the need for the playlist to be selected and played.

Scenario 6: Battery Power

Both Steve and Lisa could easily take this unit with them in the morning and use it throughout the day, which means battery power is important, so it should be able to run several hours before it needs recharging. This makes home use complicated because when they bring the unit home, they'll probably need to recharge the unit. If the batteries are low, this means the device might not be convenient to hook up to the stereo, which suggests some type of a base station that, when you drop in the unit, it not only recharges the batteries, but it also hooks up to the stereo. The problem with this idea is the computer also needs to have access to the device. This is a complex problem, but it seems likely that the computer and the stereo could compete for the device. Some decision should be made about which is the base location. Given that computers will be the source of the music that goes on the device and that most computers tend to have good speakers, I would lean toward having the base station, if one exists, be tied to the computer. This also implies that hooking the unit up to a home stereo is possible, but this probably isn't its most common use.

Scenario 7: Recording

Lisa would like to record her group in practice sessions. This implies all sorts of control issues because false starts will probably occur, which will require them to start over, or break between sections where Lisa wants to pause the recording. A classic computer approach is to start recording, then stop recording, and then delete the recording to start over. This could lead to all sorts of problems and complexities for Lisa in her ensemble. Remember, Lisa will be wrestling with a cello while she does this, so the controls must be fairly simple. Lisa will be concentrating on the music, not on the device, while she's doing this.

Because Lisa is likely to record several sessions, it also seems probable that the device should autoname the recorded tracks with something meaningful, such as Date/Time, so she knows when the recording was made. It doesn't seem likely that Lisa will want to rename the sessions on the spot, but she might want to mark one as special, so she can dig through the sea of recordings and play back those that have value to her.

Lisa is going to focus on playing her music, not setting up the recording parameters of this device. It seems clear that recording must be simple, with minimal fuss because it will be used in an environment where many other stronger social issues will be Lisa's focus. This raises the question that if recording is to be included in the device, a built-in microphone would help considerably. It might not have the quality of an external microphone, but Lisa might trade off the quality for the convenience.

In discussing this Scenario with a technical friend, he pointed out that you could never offer a Record option so simply. You would have to have compression settings because sometimes you would want to compress the sound quite a bit for voice recordings, but less for music. He raised a good point that wasn't captured initially – you could record not only music, but also voice, and there could be a large savings in disk space for the two. This raises two questions: 1) Is it worthwhile to Lisa and Steve to have this capability and 2) If so, how do we offer it?

My technical friend's suggestion of the need for multiple compression settings has "Flexibility is the root of all evil" written all over it. If this were to be offered, there should only be a Voice and a Music setting, which could be offered at record time. For the power user, the definition of what these mean could be left to the desktop software to edit.

So far, the Personas and Scenarios provide little insight into the value of this feature. It certainly sounds reasonable to be able to record meetings or lectures and the extra compression would be of big value. The bottom-line question, however, is whether this is a top-level key feature or a secondary feature to be tucked away?

Observations

The last Scenario above starts to show the limitations of Personas and Scenarios. As my Personas are clearly made up, I started wandering into the recording territory with very little basis for making sound decisions. Remember, this is an exercise to start the entire product team thinking outside the traditional features checklist mentality and to try to gain insight into what a product like this would need in the hands of a normal user. This isn't meant to replace market research, focus groups, or interviews, but it's clear this exercise has already revealed many issues and items to discuss with the full product team. At this stage, it seems clear that some type of proper research needs to take place to do more than just shoot from the hip. This doesn't invalidate the simple use of Personas at all. If it wasn't for this exercise, we wouldn't have been able to explore the space and understand the complexities that this type of product uncovers. By starting with such a "blunt tool," you can move your understanding along significantly and even increase the motivation for further research.

In running through these Scenarios, it's clear that hardware interaction seems to be a strong theme. Moving the songs to the device appears the most critical issue, but other issues such as battery life, volume, base stations, internal microphones, and FM transmitters all came out loud and clear as big issues, which could make this a truly innovative product.

A surprising outcome is this: little seems to surface on what the software should do for this product. Playing CDs and individual tracks is clearly important and some lingering issues exist in making the recordings work, but this is surprisingly light. This implies to me that the software can be significantly simplified from the current design.

This also implies something that's often found in these exercises: these Personas will use this device primarily as a tool. Broader, more personal, and social issues overshadow the use of this machine. In other words, let's not get too cute with the design.

STARTING THE DESIGN

Key Insights Are Hardware

So what is the Simplicity we're going to shoot for? As previously discussed, to fill up this device with music easily is critical or you'll lose most normal consumer types. This points to a desktop PC solution that can encode the CDs easily and download them to the hardware. The entire process needs to be as click-free as possible: insert the CD, press Copy, and off you go. Many CD programs today are close, but they make you hunt through a few too many places to get this done. This isn't all that hard to accomplish, though.

Other hardware issues exist about the volume control and the FM transmitter. The volume control is fairly straightforward and easy to get into the product. The FM transmitter is clearly one issue that requires more thought and exploration. Clear reasons exist about why this idea is potentially impractical, battery life being the most obvious one. If some creative brainstorming were done by the product team, however, this certainly appears to be a breakthrough concept that should be explored further: it implies the device is capable of playing in all the places you'd like to play music – on wireless headsets, in the car, at home, and at someone else's house.

Core Tasks

The previous hardware issues are all vital to discuss and consider for a wider product offering. For the sake of keeping this Design Break focused, though, the remaining discussion focuses on the device screen and buttons. These, too, can be vastly simplified and can make the product appear much more approachable. As to the core tasks we'd like this design to focus on, a safe bet seems that playing CDs is the core "Play" to worry about. This is exactly what we do today with most music stereo systems, so is an obvious analogue.

After that, I'd layer in playing individual tracks, followed by selecting playlists, and finally, recording new tracks. These seem to be the core tasks that must be handled in this order.

The last power-user feature was to put the settings back into the device. This last task didn't come out in our Scenario work, so it's left for last. This type of thing must be in the device because there are always things to set, but we'll make sure it goes in in such a way that it doesn't hinder the core design.

I'll admit to skipping the Priority Trick here and doing a prioritized list myself. As discussed before, one of the primary benefits of the Priority Trick is the group interaction that occurs when discussing how the various features compare.

What to Lose

The original product attempted to be a standalone device, doing everything on the small screen using its 11 tiny buttons. Examples of the breadth of tasks were making playlists, naming recorded tracks, and setting the equalizer. These are all complex tasks on such an ergonomically impoverished device and so are error prone and of extremely limited value. To gain some calm on this device and to regain some Simplicity, much of the editing must be moved off to the desktop. This would include things like creating and maintaining playlists, naming recorded tracks, and changing more complex settings. This doesn't change the fundamental features of the device at all. It simply moves the high-end complex stuff off to a place that can handle it. Make the hard, hard. This is especially true because the product can't exist without a PC, so requiring it for these advanced tasks isn't putting any additional requirement on the product.

STAGE 1

Okay. The first design stage, as shown in Figure 8-2, will be to design only a device to select and play entire CDs. As discussed in the microwave Design Break, by limiting your design to the core tasks, your design practically presents itself to you.

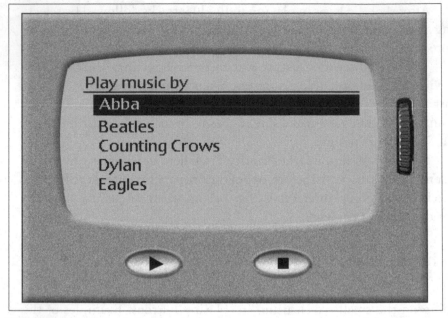

FIGURE 8-2. Stage 1 design.

The screen shows a scrolling list of artists that scrolls using the wheel on the right. Pushing the triangle Play button would then offer a similar list of scrolling albums. Pressing Play again would then start playing the CD, one track at a time. The Stop button would either stop playback or back up a level.

This first stage seems quite a good start because playing a CD only requires three controls, a far cry from the 11-plus soft buttons we started with. To be fair, though, we only do a tiny fraction of what the original design did, but what we do is now simple and obvious.

It might strike you as a bit hidden to have the Play/Stop buttons also double up as a Select/Back pair. This is a good example of how Simplicity can work to your advantage, however. Only two buttons are on the whole device. What other buttons would you push? This type of Simplicity forces users down a certain path, easily discovered and easily remembered. This is also helped by the fact that the top window is prompting the user to "Play music by" and a Play button is below the screen, so the Play button as Select is obvious.

Also notice that the design uses six lines of text instead of seven as on the original device. This allows the font to be larger, so it can be more easily read, an important consideration for all users.

This is our first design stage, capturing the core Simplicity we're trying to find. Notice how easy this was to discover as well. By focusing on a basic, but universally shared task, the design practically wrote itself.

STAGE 2

Now we have to start earning our keep, though. We need to begin layering on the additional functionality without compromising the soul of what we've discovered. The Stage 1 design covers only playing entire CDs. Now we have to add individual tracks and playlists.

The most straightforward way of doing this would be to add an additional layer to the previous design. Instead of the initial starting point being a scrolling list of artists, it will now be a scrolling list of collections: CDs, Tracks, and Playlists. It would look like the design in Figure 8-3.

Choosing CD goes into our previous Stage 1 design, Individual Track goes into a scrolling list of songs where the Play button simply plays the song. Playlist goes into a scrolling list of saved playlists where Play just plays the tracks in the same way the CDs would play.

Trade-Offs

But did you catch what just happened here? Our first layered feature has changed our precious core design! Instead of the original two levels of hierarchy, we now have three. We aren't supposed to do this! The core should stay fixed and additional functions should be layered to keep the core design whole. This example is a simple version of what can happen as you layer in additional features. Initially, when you start, you create a design that only accomplishes an extremely focused set of tasks: in this case, it was simply playing a CD collection. It should come as no surprise that, while this is a great base, it can't encompass the

FIGURE 8-3. Stage 2 design.

remainder of the functions. The power of this, however, is we now have a strong place to start. Adding the third layer of hierarchy is making the design more complex, but it's built on the same navigational model and button design that came from our initial design. In this way, the Stage 1 design had the desired effect. It started us thinking about an ultrasimple product first, which grew slightly to encompass the new functionality.

STAGE 3

Now we have to add the rest: recordings and settings. *Recordings* is the capability to record new tracks and play them back. *Settings* is where you would change more esoteric values, such as the equalizer or backlighting. The extra level of hierarchy added back in Stage 2, as painful as it was, gives us the flexibility now to add these two easily. This is a good sign our solution is working because we can easily add without changing the

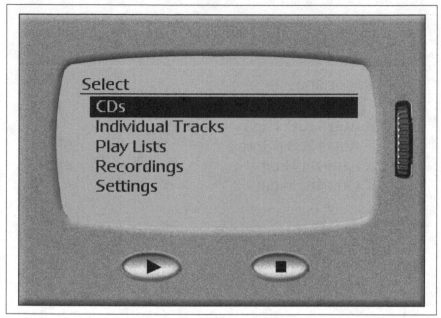

FIGURE 8-4. Stage 3 design.

design significantly. Placing them in the list at the bottom is a good way of adding depth to the product, yet keeping them naturally in a more secondary role.

However, the wording has to change slightly because we're no longer always "Playing" the items in the list. As you can see in Figure 8-4, I've changed the wording to "Select" with a plural list below it.

Recordings

The challenge will be adding in recordings without compromising the current design. In thinking about this design initially, a Record button below the screen seemed like an obvious analogue to machines today, but with the Stage 2 design in place, it was clear a new top-level button would only be of use in a small corner of the device. Once the Stage 2 design came through with only two buttons, adding a third button seemed like it would add too much weight to a high-end function. It was

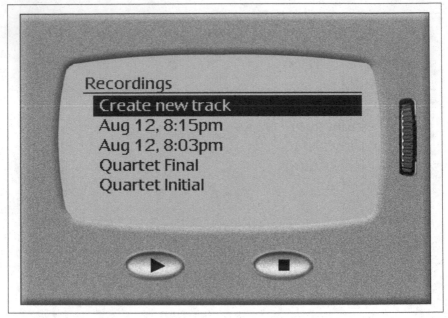

FIGURE 8-5. Adding recording.

time to make the hard, hard and to hide this feature away, as shown in Figure 8-5.

We've been developing a sense of place without realizing it. So far, each screen has had a title and contained a list of concrete items to either open or play things. The Play button takes you down and the Stop button takes you back. With this new design, this simple model is changing slightly, so I'm mixing a function with a list of items. The first item, "Create new track," would start a new recording. Everything else is simply a previously recorded track.

This is clearly trade-off territory. A physical Record button would be the more obvious thing to add, but I'm convinced the clutter of a button that might rarely be used isn't worth the trouble. I'm intentionally making this decision because we're in a higher-end corner of the device and I want to keep the gorgeously simple two-button design in tact.

But we must forge ahead and discuss what happens when the "Create new track" is selected. It came out in our recording Scenario that making a recording isn't only a matter of starting, recording a perfect song, and then pressing the Stop button. Lisa will probably have false starts or pauses in her recording. The classic technology approach would be insensitive to this and simply offer the capability to start and stop a recording. This means if a mistake were made, it would be up to Lisa to stop the recording, delete it, and then start yet another recording, which would be cumbersome. If the capability to pause existed, that might be helpful, but if they made a mistake, they'd still have a mess on their hands. Once you're aware of this problem, it's easily fixed by making the Stop button a little smarter, as shown in Figure 8-6.

This gives Lisa a choice when she presses the Stop button. Stop and Resume are the classic buttons you would expect in this situation, but I've also added Restart, which cleans up the current recording and starts from the beginning. This allows Lisa to use this device in a more realistic recording situation without adding much to the design.

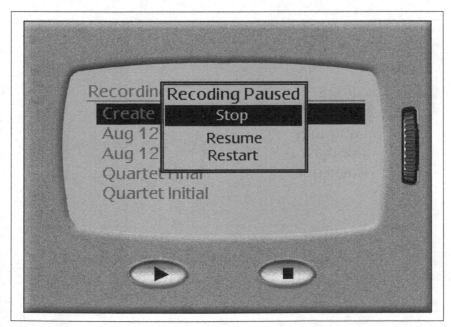

FIGURE 8-6. Improved pause.

Settings

We haven't discussed the settings on the original device, but this was a sea of many small details that Lisa and Steve would rarely need. I won't go through it here, but all the possible setting choices should be assessed using the Priority Trick to determine which ones are required for this device. The majority of the low-priority settings, if they're still needed should be set by the PC when it's connected to the device. What remains should be very simple. It would ideally be a 'choose from many' interface where the user can pick from pre-configured settings. Figure 8-7 shows the simplified settings.

For example, Equalizer should be a list of a few choices you select and nothing more. If you want to edit these choices or add another one, do it on the desktop. Much of the complexity of the original device came from the many variables in the Settings section of the device. The vast majority could be removed entirely from the product because they offered too many choices of no real value. Those that remain should be

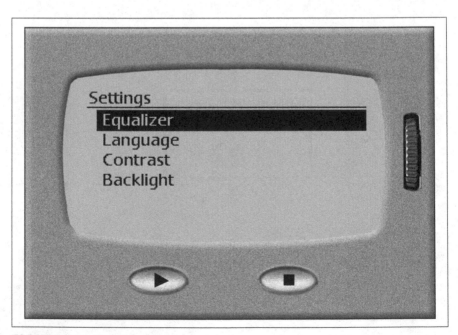

FIGURE 8-7. Simplified settings.

split into editing tasks, such as creating equalizer settings, and selecting tasks that would only offer a simple choice of a few options. This would place nearly all the complexity in the settings squarely in the PC domain, which has the interaction tools to handle these tasks much easier.

COSTS

With such a complex product, I must be careful in making cost claims. Clearly, the new design is much simpler because the number of buttons has been drastically reduced. The software would also be significantly simpler, so it would be less risky, and easier to write and debug.

Things get more complex because I shifted many requirements to the PC software, which will require some work. To be fair, this would add to the product cost. However, it seems likely that many existing products could be leveraged to take this role, so it wouldn't be as difficult as it might first appear.

In addition, the cost of the wheel scroller is also an increase, but by how much isn't clear. Given that the screen is the same, I would expect the reduction of nine buttons would cover the additional cost of the scroller. Also, please note, my scroller is a vertical wheel on the side of the display. Many versions exist of this type of input device and different placements could be used. My design is only an initial example to break away from the default idea of having an up-and-down arrow.

SUMMARY

I believe this design is shaping up fairly well. Given that we started with fairly simple Personas and some ad-hoc Scenarios, we were able to generate significant questions and issues, which have lead to an increased insight to how this product would be of value to a consumer. While we were able to make considerable headway using these ad-hoc tools, testing these ideas in a simple focus group or field study would still be useful. Many more insights would likely come from this.

Given this simple tool, however, we came up with a radically simple design, reducing the original complicated screen design, obliterating the need for soft buttons, and reducing the 11 buttons down to 2, plus a scroller and a volume control. This is clearly a much better and cheaper model than the original.

Also notice that many of the issues raised in the Scenarios would have been useful to discuss with the broader product team. Many issues could have been decided that would have significantly changed how this design proceeded. This is the real value I want you to see here — not that I was able to create a few simplified screen shots, but that I followed a simple analysis path that exposed assumptions and generated questions that would drive a team to discuss some potentially significant insights impacting the product concept. These couldn't be solved only by a designer because there would be implementation hurdles to overcome to make them a reality. By placing the product and its issues on the table with Personas and Scenarios, a much more fruitful cooperation can take place between departments that will encourage innovative thinking.

As always, this is a starting point. Much like the microwave example, I would definitely run a usability trial on this design to make sure the basic navigation works, the buttons are clearly understood, and the labels make sense. After the usability test, I would fully expect to make several changes to this design.

Innovation Blindness

One man's "magic" is another man's engineering.
"Supernatural" is a null word.

—*Robert Heinlein*

INTRODUCTION

Creating a process to guarantee innovation might seem a bit like selling a formula for turning lead into gold. There's no way I could make that attempt. But I've seen mindsets through my work that will certainly never be able to find innovation. This is what I mean by innovation blindness: attitudes that actively discourage innovative thinking.

Unfortunately, it's common that product teams don't even attempt a new, breakthrough solution. Many stick to the "style guide" approach, following the rules set down by someone else. They color within the lines. This approach definitely has merit when you're working in a well-established domain, such as a department web site within a large company. But, for such new areas as consumer electronics, few style guides exist. You have to break out and see things in new ways. Small electronic devices with onscreen scroll bars or radio buttons are clear negative examples. Just because these interaction widgets are common on a PC doesn't mean you need to place them on an MP3 player. Break out of your prison.

Innovation blindness occurs because people don't know how to question their surrounding design culture or even to entertain the possibilities that challenge this culture too strongly. If you don't know how to go about tearing down the walls – both around your project and around your ears – you're not going to break free.

But breaking through these conceptual blocks is only the first step toward innovation. The next is to implement the designs that come from breaking through these blocks. This is the second phase of innovation because breakthrough ideas don't easily transition into shipping products. Development teams, as battle-scarred veterans of many crazy deadlines, tend to refuse anything too far a field from what they know. This is a reasonable position for them to take because it often keeps unrealistic marketing requests in check. Where innovation occurs is when you get design dreamers and pragmatic programmers working together to get a brilliant design implemented with as little work as possible.

The three Insights in this chapter discuss ways through this. The first, "See the Water," is about realizing most solutions to problems are chosen from a limited default set and you have to look outside this set to get any new ideas. The second Insight, "Embrace the Impossible," is about getting the sky-high designer and the down-to-earth programmer to work together to get something that neither could have done alone. The last Insight, "Failing Fast," is about techniques in visualizing and critiquing design concepts quickly, zeroing in on an good design through iterative design.

INSIGHT 6 – SEE THE WATER

What It Is

A popular parable talks of fish not "seeing" the water. The point is, while fish live in water all the time, they never appreciate what surrounds them. Water so encompasses their life, it becomes part of the background. Water just fades away and the fish focus on more obvious things like finding food or escaping from predators.

The same is true of much of design. We're surrounded by the computer culture. Two-button mice, scroll bars, right-clicks, double-clicks, and Querty keyboards are all part of how computers are just "done."

Digital watches or any type of timer device is a prime example of this, with the tiny, single push buttons, blinking displays, and mode buttons. After you live with a certain style for a while, it becomes standard practice. It's far too easy to slip into thinking of using a "menu" here or a "Back button" there. We swim in design defaults and never realize it.

Now, nothing is wrong with design defaults. Without them, driving a car would be a nightmare. Most cars conform closely to common design, so it's fairly easy to use any car.

But we aren't designing cars, are we? We're creating new products that are exploding with new capabilities. This isn't the time for standards. This is a time to create new ways of navigating, designing products that are less cluttered and offer value without needless complexity.

This insight is more a matter of will than process. I want to make it clear that you shouldn't throw everything out the window but, more often than not, conventions are used by the uninspired as a crutch.

How to Do It

When you're developing consumer electronics, watch for these defaults. Every time you see something taken from either a desktop interface or a digital watch, question why it's there. Don't remove it; question it. These two paradigms are two of the most dominant forms of "water" that exist today. Both are entrenched approaches of how things are simply done and it's an easy trap to do something similar to their existing approach. Many consumer products have scroll bars when they don't have a mouse or even a stylus. Digital watches have doomed us to blinking modes and multiplexed mode buttons for years to come. If you're designing a small consumer product and use any of these products as a template, you have a clear case of not Seeing the Water.

You've already seen two examples of this. In the MP3 redesign, I questioned the scroll bars and had them removed. In the microwave, the digital timer was reused for the power setting and I moved the timer out into separate buttons. High-end devices tend to inherit from the desktop metaphor and low-end consumer electronics tend to inherent from the digital watch. What makes the digital watch metaphor so hard to ignore is its cost effectiveness. By having modes and reusing the display to do several different tasks, you can reduce the button count considerably. This does have the advantage of saving some money. Of course, saving production costs is a good thing, but don't let it control the design too much.

Example: E-mail on a Phone

I was working on a new design for putting e-mail into a mobile phone. Quite of bit of legacy thinking comes from how e-mail applications are done on desktop computers. The initial design had the typical folders you find on most desktop systems: Inbox, Outbox, Drafts, and Sent. This was an obvious first place to start, but we began questioning why we had such a resemblance to the desktop model. One of the first questions that cropped up was, "Why do we have so many folders?"

We made the rather obvious (in retrospect) observation that of all the items in the Outbox, Draft, and Sent folders, the vast majority were in the Sent folder. Things in the Outbox were transitory and soon ended up in the Sent folder, as did the items in Drafts. As the Outbox and Drafts items were normally small in number, it seemed much cleaner to put them all into a single super Outbox folder and mark those few with different icons. This had nice symmetry to the only remaining folder, the Inbox: massive simplification in folder structure and a much simpler model for the user.

Example: Save and Cancel on a PDA

One of my more difficult examples of not Seeing the Water was my work on a project for Symbian. This was a handheld device that used a pen for input, much like a Newton or a Palm. Early on, we made the decision this needed to act like a consumer device, not a computer, and we wanted to remove from the user experience the need for the Save button. When you closed any object in the system, it was simply saved for you.

We weren't trying to be cool and different. Good reasons were behind this decision. First, a small digital device isn't a full-blown desktop system. You aren't changing a 23-page business plan. Instead, you're changing a seven-field contact record. The need to "inform the computer it's time to write file contents out to nonvolatile magnetic storage" has long since gone.

Given that these records are so much smaller, the original protection that came from the Save dialog box no longer applies. In addition, asking users to save 35 times a day starts to get irritating. When you choose an option 99.9 percent of the time you have to ask why it is a choice at all.

Last, but not least, this no-save interaction style was already a well-established interaction paradigm. Over ten-years ago, the Newton was one of the first PDAs to adopt this approach and it was quickly adopted by the Palm. This wasn't exactly a flighty idea dreamed up on a whim. It was a working, established model.

Most of the programmers on the team, however, couldn't See this Water. As a group, they tend to love control and they couldn't get past the "but what if I make a bunch of changes and make a big mistake?" type of argument. They were so comfortable with the dominant desktop paradigm, they couldn't let go. Only after we repeatedly displayed the Newton and Palm designs did they finally start to soften. The fact that I had to push so hard shows how entrenched this type of mental inertia can be for product teams.

Things That Go Wrong

One of the more significant reasons this inertia tends to exist in design teams is for the simple reason that it isn't clear to the team that they're supposed to be creating an innovative design. Telling people to be innovative might sound odd, but many product teams will assume things must be done the "safe" way. Questioning existing design assumptions is risky and can lead to some fairly wild ideas. The team must explicitly be given permission to try some new ideas and fail at least initially. I can't stress enough how a supportive management comment in a team meeting can encourage a team's innovative attitude.

One of the bigger problems with innovative designs isn't always with the creation of the design, but in its acceptance by the rest of the company. In a time-constrained, technically fluid world, you can't blame product managers for taking the known route, if only to gain some scheduling security. This is understandable, but this isn't the environment that will create breakthrough products. Team leaders must not only encourage risk taking, but also reward attempts to break away, even if these attempts fail. In addition, an occasional thought-provoking jab, such as "Tell me why you think scroll bars are important" can sometimes jog people into Seeing the Water.

The other problem is this: making a simplification never comes free. It often has a cost. When you get a radically simpler design, you usually lose some type of information feedback or some advanced feature. In the case of the previous simplified Outbox, concern existed that people who composed many e-mails in the Drafts folder would be hurt because their items were now mixed in with other items. This was a valid concern, but it was minimized because, for the most part, people didn't create that many draft items. Those who did, could handle it. Make the hard, hard.

One more point to remember when pushing for innovation is that legacy issues are occasionally so strong, you can't break away. When working on the Newton, I designed a spreadsheet around the use of the stylus and gesture recognition. What came out of this design was a rather unique model for creating and editing formulas. Using the pen and gestures, it was much easier both to create formulas and to edit them. But this design was incompatible with Excel, the industry standard spreadsheet at the time, however. My approach was too different and it didn't meet spreadsheet users' expectations. The legacy within the spreadsheet world was strong and creating a breakaway design didn't offer enough value to be worth the switch. This was a rather naïve mistake on my part because I was ignoring some rather basic user inertia in pursuing such a radical design.

INSIGHT 7 – EMBRACE THE IMPOSSIBLE

What It Is

Conflict often exists between designers, who are good dreamers, and programmers, who are battle-scarred realists. The problem should surprise no one: they both approach their crafts from very different perspectives.

Programmers take a real beating in the designer community as the bad boys who mess up products. This is rather unfair. Programmers don't like horrible design. They are realists who want to get a product out the door. Their job is to determine how to make something ship and ship soon.

Unfortunately, good design insights get buried behind this pragmatism. When a design is reviewed by programmers, it isn't uncommon to hear, "But that would take too long to program!" This isn't because programmers are lazy. Their great strength is that they build and, having built, they have a whole raft of experiences that prove to them that life is hard, brutish, and short.

Designers, for their part, don't understand why programmers don't relax a bit and try to brainstorm. Programmers don't understand why designers don't get the sense of reality the rest of the world shares.

Assuming your simple design is well motivated by Personas and Scenarios, you should never say a design is naïve. It simply can't be implemented yet. In fact, when you find a design everyone likes, but that's technically "impossible," you have a sure-fire example of innovation staring you in the face. The trick is in determining how to ship a product that still achieves the essence of the design.

Example – Oh, That's Easy

"Impossible designs" are often perceived as a difficult technology problem, which simply can't be done. This often turns out as nothing more than a communications problem, though. Once, when I was working on a mail synchronization client for a handheld device, we had such a problem. The primary feature was to get all the e-mail off the PC and into the phone. The design called for the e-mail received on the phone, and those that came from the PC, to be merged into a single Inbox. The programming team told us this was impossible.

The problem was perception. The existing synchronization architecture was able to copy the PC e-mails over to the phone fine, but they were marked internally as "sync items" not "e-mail items," each stored into its own folder. To combine them into a single folder would cause all sorts of challenging programming problems, which would be difficult to fix. The original solution was to abandon the single Inbox and have a two-folder approach: an Inbox with e-mail items and a Synced folder with PC items.

The developers had made too narrow an assumption, thinking our design idea of a single unified folder had to be reflected in the architecture. Backing away from a technology-framed discussion, we asked how hard it would be to create a magic folder, that existed only in the Presentation layer, which took the existing Inbox and Synced folders, sorted them together, and displayed them as one. The architecture wouldn't need to change at all, we argued. The application would simply present a convenient "fiction" to the user. The developers nodded, saying, "Oh, that's easy, no problem." These guys weren't our enemies. They were simply guilty of taking our comments too literally. The idea that the Presentation layer could do some work separate from the low-level code had never occurred to them. They loved this solution because they didn't have to do anything. The application writer had to do the work and even he didn't have to do that much.

So far so good. We were making progress here. Unfortunately, our sense of calm was shattered only a few seconds later. "Oh, but wait! This won't work because you can't reply to these pretend messages in this new Inbox." They patiently explained that Sync items were a different type from the e-mail items and you couldn't reply directly to them. In the preexisting system that we were basing the new product on, the user had to choose a menu item "Convert to E-mail," which did the correct conversion magic, turning the sync item into an e-mail item, to which you could then finally reply. The answer to me was obvious: create another fiction. Show both types of items exactly the same way in the Inbox, effectively hiding the distinction from the user. If the user chose to reply to a Sync item, do the "Convert to E-mail" function on the users behalf behind the scenes, and then proceed with the reply. Their response was, "Oh, that's easy, no problem."

This is why teams need to work so closely together. The solution, the innovation, is often sitting there waiting for someone to find the fairly straightforward answer. The teams simply need to realize each group is talking a slightly different way and they need to work through a compromise that meets both needs. This example shows how design is free because we were able to get a much simpler design without it costing much at all.

How to Do It

The best way to make this work is to ensure the teams involved work together. The idea is to relax the assumptions of each side slowly, trying to find a way to implement a solution that gets as close to the goal as possible. This is where the Scenarios help. By having the teams walk through the Scenarios together, they're focused on the task, not the technology. When a technology problem occurs, you can focus on the task and ask for other solutions, some of which are capable of getting close to the ideal solution.

In the previous example, the programmers had it in their heads that I was asking for a deep architecture change, something that clearly wasn't going to happen. They couldn't separate my design from the "threat" that I was going to cost them months of work. Once they understood I didn't care how it happened, we were able to come up with the little trick that was easy and offered 100 percent of the original design.

The best trick I've learned to make this easier is to use the word "magic" as in the "magic folder." This is a bit playful, but it's effective at creating a brief suspension of disbelief, separating the programming issues, the infrastructure issues, from those in the Presentation layer. I set up the programming issues as fixed, so there's no threat to the programmers that I'm trying to change the impossible. The "magic" thing I'm trying to create exists outside the existing and unthreatened code. This establishes a safe place to brainstorm and negotiate.

Creative strategies can be discussed that use the existing infrastructure. Once the ball gets rolling, though, the door opens slightly and simple changes to the infrastructure will also be considered – small, easy-to-add things that would never have been discussed previously. This type of negotiation can be a win/win situation. This works because it places each side is a safe place and allows discussion to take place in a neutral space.

This trick is a good starting point, but it doesn't guarantee success. Embracing the Impossible works best when both sides have built up a good working relationship and trust each other's abilities. Not only does the programmer have to bend and creatively work out ways to make the design work, but the opposite is also true. The designer must trust the programmer when something just isn't going to work. It shouldn't be a surprise that designs can be too aggressive: a subset of the original design is often enough. When you get this type of give-and-take, you can truly get some creative work because you have an informed design working with creative technology to get a solution that transcends both disciplines.

Example – Bluetooth

At the beginning of this book, I gave an example of a mobile phone with a wireless headset based on the Bluetooth standard. This came from a real project I was working on. Initially, I wanted all devices to be discovered automatically by the phone and to eliminate that rather complex control panel. I pushed hard, working with the team to see if an "Oh, that's easy" solution was hiding in there somewhere. Unfortunately, the problem was complex and my wonderful magic fix was clearly not going to happen. I ended up relaxing my requirements only to worry about the headset that came in the box. In effect, for the first generation of the product, this would be the only type of device that was available, so solving the general case didn't hurt the product in the short run.

Once I agreed to solve only the headset case, we were then working on a smaller problem, one which was much easier to solve. The horrible control panel was kept in, but only as a backup for the secondary devices that might come up. I was a bit crushed that a broader solution didn't occur but, in this case, by relaxing the design ambition, we were able to get a solution that was still effective for the broadest Scenario. This doesn't mean my original design was bad. It simply wasn't practical for the first release, so I had to settle for a much-reduced version that handled most of what I wanted.

Things That Go Wrong

The biggest reason things sour between designers and programmers is because both sides get locked into their own solution. The discussion quickly becomes a version of "Why can't you see it my way?" The best solution here is to step back and focus on the Persona and the Scenario. Go back to the task that motivated the design. By backing up this far, you can usually find a common ground where both parties can agree. Separating design from technology is the first step. The next step is to relax each side's thinking and try to find a common ground that achieves as much of the design as possible.

Another problem is a programmer's natural inclination to see any programming as a deep architectural solution that must be able to grow into the future. Of course, this type of thinking is correct and should generally be encouraged, but not on every single thing you do. By relaxing the need to make something architecturally pure, you can often find a common ground that will get a solution out the door, yet still offer the design you need. The best way to discover this type of solution is to ask, "Are you assuming some deep architectural change here, which might not be necessary?" This usually provokes a worthwhile conversation.

An equivalent problem is the designers' insistence that they have discovered truth and beauty in their design, and anything less is completely unacceptable. There are times when what is designed just isn't possible. Ways through this situation are to ask the designer these questions: "What are your key concerns here? Is this part of your design a core task? Are there other ways we can meet this need?" Again, the purpose is to get both sides to relax and try to meet in the middle.

INSIGHT 8 – FAIL FAST

What It Is

Creating breakthrough designs is a terrible cross to bear. No one can conjure up a breakthrough design on the spot, but approaches exist that can help significantly. I often find it useful to think of design as a process of "criticizing your way to a solution." When you're just starting, or possibly, when you're stuck at some point in the design, write down a solution, any solution, as a means of getting something going. It will certainly be wrong, but that isn't the point. By putting pen to paper, you visualize your problem, shifting out of the logical/verbal space into the creative/visual space. With your problem in front of you in a different way, you can then talk about why it's wrong, what aspects of it are good, what improvements could be made, and so on.

I call this approach to design *Failing Fast*, which is a significant shift in approach and creative liberty. Early on in a project, I make it clear to the team that we have to run through hundreds of bad designs before we find something amazing. Through bad designs you are able to understand the problem, the constraints, and types of solutions.

I'm assuming you've already done your homework and completed most of the steps in the previous chapters. Use this Insight when you're past the homework stages and starting to design actively. Many designers get brainlock and, sometimes, can't move forward. By removing the stigma of suggesting only perfect solutions, you can start to think outside the box, suggesting odd, even weird solutions that everyone knows are wrong. But every time you express a solution, your mind can't help but analyze and ponder. Usually, every time you do a bad sketch, you get a little closer to understanding what you do want.

Failing Fast can occur at many levels in the design. I find Failing Fast most useful early on when I'm just starting to formulate the initial design concepts, but this can also continue into the more refined and final stages of design. I use three fairly well-known techniques to do this: Sketching, Interactive Demos, and User Testing. These tools are effective, not only for design, but also for project management because they're compact and effective communication tools when working across the product team.

Technique 1 – Sketching

Sketching is my thinking tool of choice. When I'm stuck I start sketching, quick and messy. I must point out that my sketches are *ugly*. I don't have the natural drawing talent that can draw perspective and shading. The type of sketching I'm talking about is what anyone can do. It can be nothing more than boxes, lines, and scribbled words. The key wonder of sketching is it gets you out of rational word mode and starts putting you into two-dimensional design mode.

Problems that block you start looking different when you sketch them. You notice how busy something will be or that when you lay it out horizontally, the buttons look better on the top. Sketching enables you to get down what you think you know, and then discover problems or insights through visual inspection.

Example: Web Sketch

Figure 9-1 is an example sketch I did when designing a web site. It was to have three major sections: a calendar, a messages area, and a contact list. I had already done my Scenario, Persona, and Priority work, so I had a good idea of who was going to need what. My sketches were simply a fast brain dump and quickly revealed some flawed thinking on my part.

The first thing I noticed was the varying layout styles. My approach to messaging was horizontal with the top pane for a message list and the bottom for each message's content. Contacts was a fairly vertical approach and Calendar looked like it could go both ways. My work on unFeatures has always shown me that people need a strong sense of place when using any product. It's useful to design different views to have consistent layouts. As the user goes from view to view, he or she can focus on the task and the data, not on wondering where to look.

As each view required a list of items, and then details on that item, it seemed reasonable to have the lists have a similar presentation. This would help the user, who after learning one view can transfer this to another view. This pushed me into considering making all the views vertical in layout, not the current mixture I had sketched.

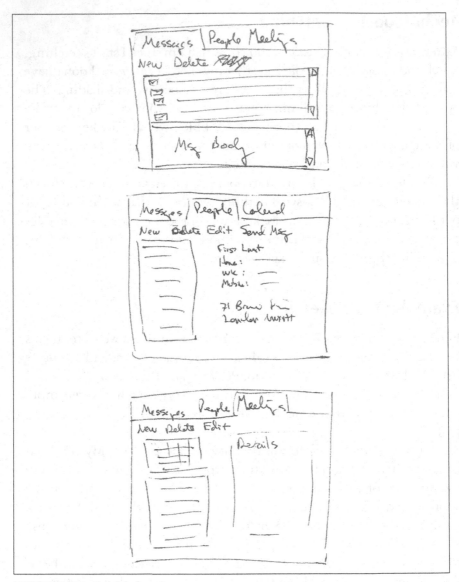

FIGURE 9-1. Initial sketches.

Now it became quite clear there was a reason desktop e-mail clients have a horizontal layout. So much information must be displayed in the "message list": subject, who sent it, the date, the time, the size, and so forth that moving to a vertical set of panes was clearly going to be a problem. My vertical layout seems to have failed.

But this insight drove me further because my previous work clarified this wasn't going to be a typical desktop e-mail client. It was more like a mobile phone messaging client, which normally shows only the name of the sender. This lead me to See the Water and understand that the desktop horizontal layout was a design default, which didn't apply here, and I could break out of its grip. This pushed me back into a vertical layout with careful consideration for exactly what had to be in each pane.

I also continued with the Calendar view, but I was fairly confident I had a good start. Each view would have a strongly vertical layout with a list of items to select on the left and with the details of each item on the right. This began to feel like I was on the right track.

By doing a few simple sketches, I effectively blundered into my design defaults and how they created a layout inconsistency. Fixing this consistency created immediate problems as well, but that, too, was easily fixed because of my previous user homework. Quite an effective return for a few scribbles.

Increasing Fidelity

The early sketches are fast because you have so many things to discover, you don't want to waste time and fail slowly. My early sketches are rough. I'll even draw some text as a wavy line because it usually doesn't matter. Once I firm up my understanding of where I want to go, though, I try to make some cleaner sketches, with a better layout. I draw out the text properly. If I'm feeling really confident, I start putting the sketches into a drawing or paint program to start getting layout issues and font sizing down.

What's nice about all the these approaches is they're still about 1,000 times faster than writing code. Not only that, I can sketch independently of technology concerns. I can image the impossible solution and get it down without having programmatic constraints filter it too early.

I stay with paper sketches for a while, even taking cleaned-up versions to a few meetings and discussing them with various members of the team. Pen-and-paper sketches are obviously trial concepts. When discussing them with people, the conversation stays focused on the big issues. If you were to present a design done in Photoshop, you'd certainly

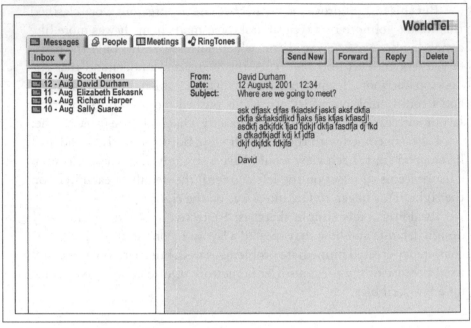

FIGURE 9-2. Higher fidelity sketching.

get such comments as "Why is that button blue?" and "Those icons are too small." At this early stage in the design, you want to answer the big infrastructure and Task layer questions. Color and icon size belong in the Presentation layer and should be left until much later.

Having explored extensively using only paper and pen, I then move on to cleaning it up. The computer sketches shown in Figure 9-2 were done in a drawing program. Even though this is much slower than pencil sketching, it's still fairly quick. This example was done in about an hour. The purpose of moving to a higher-fidelity form of sketching is I can explore font and layout issues better. Scribbled buttons that easily fit on my drawing become much too wide for the screen. The 12 lines of text turn out to be only 6 lines in reality.

Both paper sketches and computer drawings are simple, but effective tools to use when communicating between groups. When working on a design, I show my sketch to the technical lead and ask for his input. He can see where I'm coming from and we can discuss high-level issues quickly. This type of simple approach is effective at setting up "Embrace the Impossible" type of meetings. By sharing ideas early and in rough-sketch form, you can build a common understanding that gets you both working and thinking the same way.

Sketching is also a great tool because it's so egalitarian. Everyone can draw boxes and write words. In fact, sketching is a useful tool for designers and programmers to use, so they can find a common means of communicating. Often when I discuss issues with a programmer, I hand over the pencil and ask him to draw out what he means. This usually surprises him, but by asking for a drawing, we create a joint concept between us, one that doesn't represent his view or mine, but a joint view between us. This can make a great difference in lowering barriers.

Technique 2 – Interactive Demos

Interactive demos are only a fancy version of sketches. They're one more step in increasing the fidelity. At Symbian, I had three full-time people doing nothing but writing interactive demos. The tool of choice was Director because it was the dominant tool at the time. Flash is coming on strong right now because its development tools have become stronger. I've even used PowerPoint successfully to stitch together a series of static screen shots.

Interactive demos are particularly valuable if you're working with a concept that requires real data, such as a list of names to scroll through or meetings to browse. You can test concepts that would be months away if you were using a real programming language. When I was consulting at American Express, a product required a connection to a mainframe. This would have meant weeks of work simply to get it communicating, but I could mock up a dummy screen in an hour with Director.

As you drive your prototyping from sketches to screen shots to interactive demos, your product concept becomes more and more refined. It also becomes more and more fixed. Don't go to interactive demos until you're ready. You should have exhausted what you can do with sketches first. Demos are more like programming than drawing, so they can take longer and slow your cycle time. You definitely want to use demos because they're many times faster than code, but that's still much slower than sketches.

Much like paper sketches, interactive prototypes are effective in showing other teams what you're thinking about. You can produce them fairly quickly, and then get a chance to explain your approach and the key concerns in a compact form.

Technique 3 – User Testing

User testing is a deep topic that has been written about extensively. There are recommended books in the appendix at the back of the book. Many companies already know about and do user testing. My comments here aren't about the technique, as much as the use of it as a tool for team communications.

User testing is, at its core, a means of criticism. As such, it is useful in Failing Fast. You use it when you think you have a solution and you want to validate it. You discover such things as whether a design works, what surprising problems the design has, and if the design is capable of enabling users to accomplish the high-priority tasks well.

What most people don't appreciate is that you can user test the paper sketches I discussed previously. These are called *paper prototypes* because you only need a few pieces of paper to show the various states of the design. The user speaks out loud, saying, "I'll click this button now" and you pull out the correct sketch from your pile and place this in front of him. This isn't a classical usability test but it can still determine some clear problems or misconceptions. I've gone from problem, to design, to test, to report in a single day. This sounds fast, but a growing "Guerilla Usability Testing" movement is forming, originally proposed by Jacob Nielson. This movement has made a strong point that less is more. Testing a design with only four to six users can often find the majority of a design's problems. This doesn't mean no place exists for formal usability tests, but when you're in early product concept development, these quick tests using small groups of participants and rough paper-based prototypes are fast and cost-effective. This type of usability testing is effective at Failing Fast because you can discover issues with real users early in the product concept.

This is the hidden power of user testing, which is effective on simple versions of your product, not the nearly final beta code. By then, the product is too far gone to make many changes. Fixing a sketch isn't hard at all.

Once a company begins to understand the power of user testing, it starts to enhance the shared understanding I keep mentioning. By asking about and tracking user-testing reports, management becomes aware of where the design is and what issues are cropping up. This is a fairly simple means to get others involved in the design problem.

Things That Go Wrong

If user testing isn't properly motivated, however, it can go wrong. I've seen political situations where two competing designs are on the table and someone suggested both designs be user tested to determine which one is better. User testing isn't a weapon. Too often, user testing is used as a means of choosing between Option A or B. This is ineffective because Option C, which is better than either A or B, is always available.

In addition, you only get criticism from user testing. Extracting value judgments is difficult. A good user test will point out problems in both Option A and Option B. Of course, if one option works perfectly and one is a failure, then you can choose. Most of my experience has shown you'll find many problems with both Options A and B, however, so you won't be able to make that choice as easily as you might think.

The other problem with traditional usability testing is it's too academic and slow. Classic tests historically ran 20 users through an exercise with task timings and statistical analysis. This type of test can, indeed, be valuable in looking for problems in a well-established design, but it has a high time and monetary cost. The point of Failing Fast is to iterate the design frequently. Classic tests can take well over a month to plan, run, and report. Four Guerilla Usability tests could be run in less time and cost less.

CONCLUSION

Innovation isn't easy to quantify. As I mentioned in the beginning, it's hard to tell you how to do it, but there are many ways to mess it up. In general, what I find in some companies is a "barely coping" type of plan, where all they want to do is make the next deadline. The idea that you should push the envelope and try to visualize the impossible seems a frivolous waste of time.

What makes innovation work is making it fearless and fast. By giving the team some time to work through new ideas, you have a chance to discover something that will not only be innovative, but also could save you some significant development time.

The first insight, See the Water, is the Zen insight – trying to break out of the assumptions that pin you down. The next insight, Embrace the Impossible, acknowledges the seeming impossibility of the designs created by proper user-centered design. However, it is by embracing impossible problems that you foster innovation. The last insight, Failing Fast, is about the hard-nosed persistent aspect of creation. Just do something, do anything, and watch it fail. You'll usually learn quite a bit in the process. Innovation doesn't flow fully formed through your fingers on to the paper. It only comes in fits and starts, and, sometimes, you have to work your way through dozens of designs to find your way to the one that pulls it all together.

Design Break: Heater Timer

Increasingly, people seem to misinterpret complexity as sophistication, which is baffling – the incomprehensible should cause suspicion rather than admiration. Possibly this trend results from a mistaken belief that using a somewhat mysterious device confers an aura of power on the user.

—*Niklaus Wirth*

PROBLEM

This Design Break will rewrite a commercially available heater timer. Early feedback on the book indicated this example was far too boring. However, the Insight "See the Water," discussed in the previous chapter, is a classic problem and this product is a perfect example. By understanding this design dead-end, you can see and fix this style of problem many times over.

At first glance, this beast is a little grim and practically screams complexity. A plumber who installs this unit joked that while some of the kids could use it, none of the adults could. In fact, most of the time, no one ever bothered to change the default settings the plumber set up on installation! This is a powerful admission. The device is so complex it usually isn't used. It might as well be a white box with no controls of any kind. This is the type of product that mystifies and frustrates consumers.

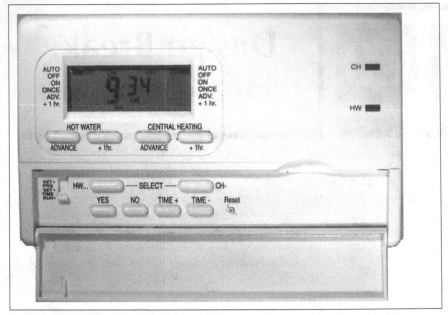

FIGURE 10-1. Initial product.

We're going to take this design apart and put it back together again. The major focus will be on innovation issues, both discovering them and brainstorming solutions. Numerous trade-offs will need to be made.

Brief Introduction to Boiler Timers

For those of you who haven't experienced radiator heating, let me briefly introduce you. This device controls the heating of the boiler for both the hot water and the radiator heating system. Keeping the boiler running all day is rather expensive, so this device turns it on and off with a clock timer to coincide with you being home. This usually means turning it on for a few hours in the morning and again in the evening. In addition, this device also controls the heating of the house because, in the summer, you want to have hot water, but you want the radiator heating off.

Original Design

The original design not only has many tiny buttons, but the LCD also has numerous little labels/icons hidden around the perimeter such as ON, OFF, MTWTF, and YES/NO. All in all, more that 40 items/states/types of information exist, which the user must parse to understand the current state of the system. (See Figure 10-1.)

To use this device, you must understand two different task models: programming and using. To program the device, you have to open the door at the bottom, slide the switch on the left from RUN to SET PRG. Once you do this, you descend into a serial path of choices offered to you on the LCD display that set the 16 timers necessary to make the device work. The details are a bit painful but, to give you an idea, simply to review the current timer settings, I have to push a combination of the YES and NO button 24 times. If I get it wrong, I can accidentally overwrite my program because, in addition to browsing the setting, a COPY? question occasionally appears on the screen, offering to copy the settings from one timer to the next.

Once programmed, to use the device, you must push the ADVANCE buttons for the hot water and the central heating. For example, if I'm leaving on vacation and want to turn the unit off, I have to push the ADVANCE button for hot water five times to advance its state to the OFF indicator and the same number of presses for the central heating.

If I want a little extra heat in the evening (if I'm staying up late), I have to use the two ADVANCE buttons to move the indicator to the +1 hr spot. If I advance the CH indicator (Central Heating) but not HW (Hot Water), I get no effect because I'll only circulate cold water through the radiator. Making a mistake with this design is extremely easy.

Single Interaction Track

When programming the device, you need to program both the hot water and the central heating timers. Each can be started and stopped twice a day. This gives a total of eight timers to set for a single day. The following (Figure 10-2) is the flowchart of the process I had to go through to simply review the current settings:

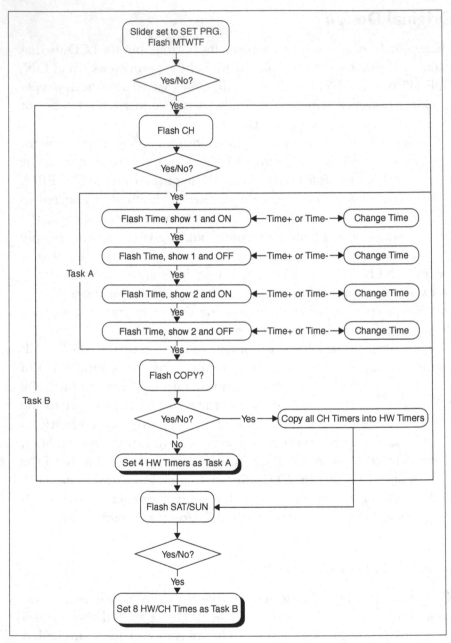

FIGURE 10-2. Original task flow.

Notice the shorthand I used to make this flow possible to fit it on only one page. The shadowed boxes refer to the previous task groupings. For me to review all timers, I had to go through Task B two times and Task A four times. This process is a complex mix of capability. Not only can you view the timer values, but you can set them and even copy values to other days. To do all this functionality, you only have four buttons: YES, NO, TIME+, and TIME−. This is a limited interaction space so, to compensate, the device has to lead you through an interrogation, which you must answer correctly and precisely to get through the gauntlet of options. It's easy to press the wrong button accidentally and copy over the entire weekend timers, when you were only interesting in reviewing the current settings.

ANALYSIS

Persona

Before we start the redesign, let's do our homework and create a target Persona. Let's imagine Emma, married to David, mother of two children, ages 8 and 10. Emma works part-time as a secretary at a life insurance company and she arrives home in time to greet the kids when they return from school in the late afternoon. Her family gets up early on weekdays to get ready for school and comes home around 4 P.M. David also works and leaves for work about the same time as Emma, but returns a few hours later.

What type of details do we know about Emma? She is a whiz at her word-processing package and can do simple spreadsheet work. Whenever anything goes wrong with the network or her printer, however, she calls the support people. Emma has a cell phone, but she only has three numbers on it: home, work, and David's phone. She has a hectic schedule with getting the kids ready for school in the morning — the morning rush is always crazy. Weekends can be even crazier, with everyone rushing in all directions on Saturday. Even Sunday is a bit odd because, even though it might be a bit lazy, something usually must be coordinated.

A sample schedule of times when heat would be important to Emma would be the following:

- ▣ Waking up early in the morning, so Emma can dress the kids for school.

- ▣ Taking bathes at night.

- ▣ During the rare day when David has to stay home with a sick child.

- ▣ On a rainy Saturday, when everyone is stuck indoors.

- ▣ When the winter gets colder, the heat needs to stay on longer to keep the house warm.

What does this product offer Emma? The whole purpose of this device is to save Emma money. The device will automatically turn off the heat when Emma and her family are gone. Although she could do this with a manual control, this could create two potential problems: 1) switching off a manual control is easy to forget, and 2) the house is cold when Emma returns home. The device offers to fix these two problems, and Emma should get better comfort and increased heating savings.

What are Emma's goals for this product? At the highest level, Emma doesn't want it to complicate her life. If this device makes her house too cold too often, it won't be worth the trouble. If the device accomplishes Emma's highest goal, then the secondary goal of saving money will be worth the effort.

Scenarios

Scenario 1: Setup

When the product is first installed, Emma would like to set the device to match the schedule of her family. The first issue this raises is that Emma doesn't have a schedule that can be carved in stone. The weekday mornings seem stable, but the weekends can vary. On some days, they take off early, while on other days, they want to sleep late. This seems to point out that Emma might need to tweak this schedule frequently. She'll certainly need to change it when winter comes because she'll want to have the heat stay on longer.

This seems to point out that the setup isn't a one-shot action but, instead, is something that will be continually tweaked throughout the use of the product. This strongly suggests that editing the timer settings must be visible and simple to do.

In addition, it seems unlikely that Emma will ever care about turning on the heat at 3:18 P.M. Some time after 3 P.M. will probably be close enough, which gives us some flexibility in setting the time; a completely to-the-minute setting doesn't appear to be required.

Scenario 2: Staying at Home

On occasional days, such as a day at home with a sick child, someone will be home all day. There must be a way to turn the heat on easily for that entire day. And it would be nice if Emma didn't have to change the Master Schedule because the heat could easily be left on the following day.

This points to a need to make the device have an ALL DAY type of button, where the heat can be turned on for this special instance, but then have the schedule return to normal the following day.

Scenario 3: Vacation

When Emma's family leaves on vacation, there must be a way to turn everything off. It would be nice if this didn't change the normal schedule.

Scenario 4: Summer/Winter

It isn't always cold. When spring comes, Emma will want to turn off the heat, but to keep the hot water.

These Scenarios give us a good starting point as to how this design would be of value to Emma. The following priority core tasks seem to come from this:

1. View and set the timer schedule easily.

2. Turn on the heat for a single day.

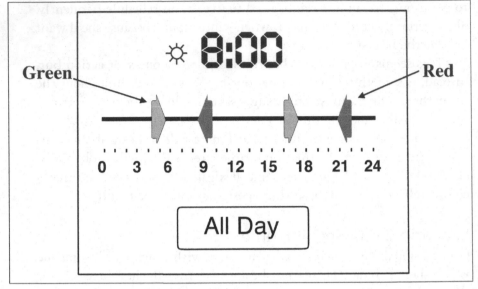

FIGURE 10-3. Stage 1 design.

3. Go on vacation.

4. Turn off the radiators.

As I said before, this is a tool to get us thinking: it doesn't replace classic user research. What we have so far, though, seems like a good start. This work is probably more focused than what many companies do today when they're creating a product, so even this work would make a significant impact on the products they create. Let's see where this takes us.

STAGE 1 – FIND THE CORE

Let's start with a core design. This design should be able to set the time for the heat to turn on and be able to set the heat to run all day when everyone is at home. Figure 10-3 is my first sketch of what this could look like. I'm not taking time making this extra pretty – this is only a quick layout to get a rough idea. This was put together in a few minutes.

The digital clock is at the top, so the time is always visible. This enables Emma to have a rough idea when the timer is about to turn on or off. An LED that lights up when the heat is on is next to the timer, so Emma has easy confirmation that everything is working. This type of extra feedback is useful to Emma because she can tell at a glance that the heat is definitely on.

There are two pairs of sliders: one for the morning and one for the evening. By putting them on a single slider, you get the day at a glance. The left slider of the pair is green and the right slider is red. These colorings are an initial thought to indicate START/STOP times. This might not work in user testing, but it seems like a good starting concept. This single slider has another subtle, but important, design: it makes setting up overlapping timers, which was an error condition in the original design, impossible.

The time is set with a 24-hour clock because this was assuming a European market, but it could easily be changed to A.M./P.M. Notice I didn't use an analog clock, which is definitely worth considering. The main reason I chose this clock is because it matched the number on the slider a bit better, but I'm not firm on this decision. I could go either way.

Beneath the slider is an "All Day" button, which will turn on the heat for the day. It should have some feedback, such as an embedded LED, so Emma has confirmation when it's pushed that the heat will be on during the day. Notice this allows Emma to turn the "All Day" button off if she changes her mind.

This design seems like a good start. As I discussed earlier in the book, when you get this type of Simplicity, you drive understanding. So few choices exist on this design, that it's hard to be confused by an array of buttons. By limiting the choice, you provide obvious use.

The huge secondary win to this simple design is not only does it give immediate feedback about the current settings, but it also invites Emma to tweak the settings easily. She can increase the settings slightly when the weather gets colder or even experiment by turning off the heat a little earlier to see if it makes a difference. You can imagine elements that "had to be" part of the original timer design, such as separate timers for the weekend, can be a simple button push, which is so simple, it isn't required anymore. Simple designs that can be completely understood, and in addition make the customer feel in control, are perceived as more powerful and useful. And this design puts Emma in control.

STAGE 2 – EXPAND THE CORE

As with the previous Design Breaks, we now have the core design. The next step is to layer in the additional features. Notice, though, that following this problem from Emma's perspective has led to a large change in the product model from the original design. Initially, a concept existed of setting the boiler separate from the heating. You not only had to change the timers for these two separately, but you also had to indicate which one was running or turned off. This distinction is completely gone with this design. The model here is more of a Turn It On or Turn It Off model. This clearly is a bit too simplistic and we'll fix that later. This is the type of approach that makes sense to Emma, however.

So, in this new expanded design, we have to add, an On/Off switch for vacations, a way to turn off the heat during warm weather, and a means to set the clock time.

The vacation switch is rarely used and should definitely be pushed off to the side, so it doesn't interfere with the core design. A simple On/Off switch on the side or hidden behind a little door at the bottom of the unit would work fine.

As to HW/CH stuff, the original design was much too complex because its only value was to turn the central heating off in the summer. A single Summer/Winter switch cuts to the chase. This leads up to the more functionally complete design in Figure 10-4.

The choices on the bottom would be hidden under the swinging door panel, much like the one in the original design. The On/Off switch is straightforward, but I chose a more verbose labeling for the Summer/Winter switch to keep its function more self-describing.

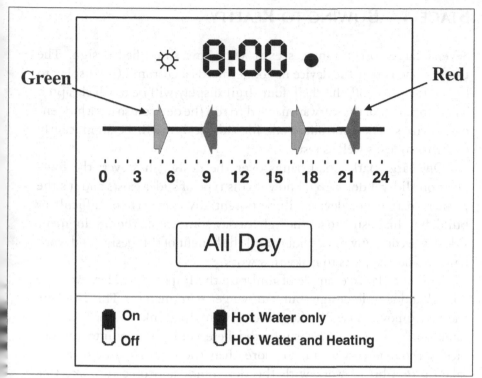

FIGURE 10-4. Stage 2 design.

One last addition is a watch stem next to the digital clock to set the time. Because we have no other use for the display than to have it be a clock, we don't need any of that Set mode nonsense. If you spin the stem, the time changes. End of story.

Of course, I'd run a quick usability study on the design to make sure it works. I'd be sure to be sensitive to insights gained, understanding users goals, the clarity of labels – especially something like All Day, which I would easily change if there were problems understanding it – and whether the slider concept seems to get its point across.

Assuming the design makes it past this gauntlet, it seems to be philosophically correct. This design is practically usable right out of the box because all you must do is spin a dial to set the time and it will start doing something reasonable.

STAGE 3 – BOWING TO REALITY

Several large cost advantages exist with this simplified design. The biggest one is that the device no longer needs a custom LCD display to be built: a plain, off-the-shelf, four-digit display will be much cheaper. The Simplicity of the software needed to run the device also has a hidden-cost savings. The controller code for this design will be significantly easier to code, as well as test.

One large dark cloud hangs over the design, however: the four-position slider. I don't even know if this type of slider exists and it's the primary reason this device will be potentially expensive or difficult to build. For this design to see the light of day, someone on the development side of the company must understand the benefit of this design and work hard to find the parts to make this work.

This is a classic example of Embrace the Impossible. Here we have a good and simple design, but can we get it to market? This is where the real innovation will take place. I want to think this part can be found and all the changes suggested here could be put into the device without it costing much more than the original. But it would take quite a bit of work with the development people to make this possible.

To make this Design Break more interesting, however, let's assume nothing goes right and the development hurdles are valid. How does the team Embrace the Impossible and keep the essence of the design even though nothing seems to be going our way? Let's go through some of the more aggressive design elements and assume they aren't possible. We'll try to keep the original design concept intact, even though we're forced to use a more conservative approach.

The Watch Stem

The watch stem is a beautifully simple way to set the time. I'd like to keep this if at all possible. However, a stem will probably cost more that two Up/Down push buttons. You could replace the stem with these buttons and not lose too much. You have that horrible digital experience of pushing 17 times and accidentally holding it down so it goes into Autorepeat mode, and then overshoots your target time. But setting the time isn't a frequent task, so we could survive this.

The All-Day Button

The All-Day button isn't aggressive, it's the On/Off light that can cause trouble. The lighted All-Day button could be replaced with a plain, unlighted button with an LED next to it, but that probably won't save much. One of the obnoxious costs in a product like this is mounting something into the case. One trick we could try is to mount the LED on the motherboard near the push button and build the case out of translucent material. Turning on the All-Day button could turn on the internal LED, making it glow through the plastic. OK, this is a little wacky, but once you know what you want, you can have these types of brainstorms to keep the concept intact.

A physically locking push button doesn't work because, at the end of the day, it has to "pop" out again. About the only trick I can come up with is to reuse the On LED button next to the clock. When the user pushes the All-Day button, the LED starts to blink. I'd be grumpy about this change because it abstracts the LED between two different functions, so it's possible the user won't get it. The blinking is fairly obvious and in their face though, so a good cause/effect is going on here. This is a second-best solution, but one that could work. I'd like to user-test this idea to be sure.

The Door

The nice part of the door at the bottom is it clearly shows what is primary and what is secondary to the device. The new design is so much simpler, even the door could go. I'd rather not lose it, though, because it clearly separates the two worlds, but we could make it work. Possible changes to the design would be to make the bottom two switches look diminutive to keep the primary/secondary effect working. Putting these switches on the side of the case might also be possible.

The Timing Slider

This is the tough one. What are our choices? The key choice is to keep the interaction direct. You could break the slider into four dials: one pair for setting the Start/Stop time of the morning timer and the other pair for the evening timer. You'll get a clunky 2×2 grid, but at least you can still view/change the settings directly. The only problem here would be to have all 24 hours available and legible on the dial labels. Figure 10-5 shows this design now makes it easy to have an error: the user can now set overlapping times, with the morning stopping after the afternoon starts.

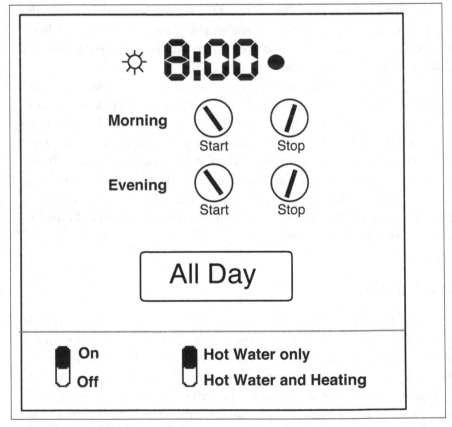

FIGURE 10-5. Dials to set time.

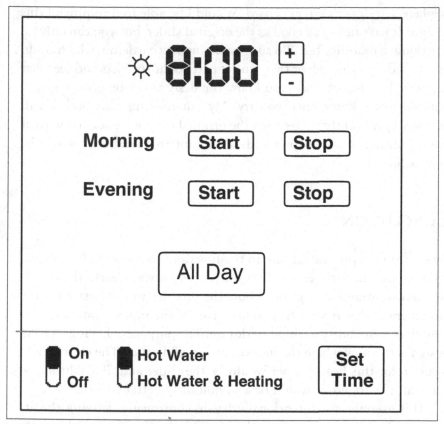

FIGURE 10-6. Reduced cost design.

The classic digital approach to this problem would be to reuse the digital clock to view and edit the timer settings. This is a serious compromise because the beauty of the original design was that everything was visible at a glance. Figure 10-6 shows how this would look.

We now have to "share" the digital display, so buttons must get you into and out of using the display. Morning Start will blink the digits and you can set them, pressing Start again would then "set" the time. This is a clear departure from the original design. It, too, has the same error potential as the dial design in Figure 10-5.

This design will clearly be cheaper than the slider model because it replaces its more complex part with only five simple push buttons. This is where a designer's job gets hard. Would I be able to recommend this design? It isn't nearly as good as the original slider, but you can only do one thing: a usability test. I'd suggest an interactive demo, which could be mocked up in a week or two. Run it past about six users and see what happens. If it passes, then you know the design will be good enough, but you won't know until you try. My gut tells me this design will perform significantly better than the original design we started with at the beginning of the chapter and, if only for that reason, it would be worthwhile.

Conclusion

By starting simple and adding in the functions, we were able to create a simple design fairly easily. This initial design was clearly the breakthrough we were looking for in how the product would best meet the customer's needs. It was the potential cost of the innovation that challenged, the capability to ship this design. The purpose of having an ideal design is to know where the innovation can add value. The clear area to focus on for this heater timer would be the slider and, if a solution to this could be found, it would be a significantly better design.

This exercise was intentionally harsh, continually denying the attempts at finding an innovative solution. This does happen and designers must be able to cope with this. By keeping the breakthrough design in mind, you can discuss the second and third best solutions that get as close as possible to this idealized design. Shipping these degraded designs because of cost constraints is still an honorable place to be. Seeing the light and getting tantalizingly close to the perfect design, and then having to back off, might be frustrating, but it's important to remain humble as a designer and realize the world won't always give your ideas the wheels they need.

Implementation Blindness

The spirit was willin', but the body was weak.
—*Gospel Spiritual*

INTRODUCTION

The Last Blindness

Curing user and feature blindness is about doing your homework to understand who your target is and what are the core things your target needs to do. You start creating designs that meet this core need and only then layer on the more advanced functions. Curing innovation blindness is about having the courage and teamwork to find a means to implement these new, simpler designs. *Implementation blindness*, the last blindness, is about making sure these designs make it out the door. Many companies don't even try to find Simplicity and this is frustrating to me. What I find heart breaking is companies that do try, but seem to lose it along the way. Curing implementation blindness is about keeping your vision on track.

Most designers have a slightly naïve belief that all the hard work in creating a product is only in getting the initial design completed. I, too, fall into this trap because the complete design is such a major milestone, it's understandable you should want to rest for a while once it's finished.

Unfortunately though, the real work is about to begin. This design has to run a technical, political, and managerial gauntlet that can pick away at the design until what makes it out the door is a pale shadow of the original design. The birthing pains of product delivery always seem to fade and I relearn this truth again and again. The last 10 percent always seems to take 90 percent of my energy because the soul of a design will wither and die if it isn't ruthlessly protected and guided through the development cycle.

Yin/Yang Design

The central theme in curing implementation blindness is understanding natural tensions occur in any product team. Marketing, design, development, and project management, to only name the big four, have different ways of valuing and solving problems. As a product begins nearing completion, pressures mount to get it out quickly to reach date, time, and cost targets. That the original design never makes it through to the end unscathed is nearly always the case.

At this stage, well-intentioned, but naïve, decisions can be made that will make the product sink or swim. Trying to keep everything in the product can create delays that will kill the product launch. Jettisoning too many features will kill the product's viability. How can anyone navigate this mine field?

The solution is fairly obvious, but rarely occurs: have the teams work together. I assume by this point, this statement shouldn't surprise you. You need all the skills and approaches to work together. You need to use both the yin with the yang of the product team; otherwise, you're not using the skills you have effectively.

In addition to working together, I suggest you work together early, rather than late, in the project. When you don't have time, making good decisions is difficult. Good decisions are usually early decisions. Because most companies don't Fail Fast, as discussed in the previous Insight, they only discover their communication problems right before the product ships and, by then, it's much too late.

Yet, time and time again, I see companies where marketing throws a feature list over to the design department, which then creates a design that's thrown over the wall to development. Much like the children's game "telephone," where whispers are passed from one person to the next, what comes out at the end has little resemblance to the original. Too many assumptions fall apart, goals aren't shared, or decisions are considered naïve by the programmers. This process creates a house of cards that will cause nothing but product-planning grief.

Design Artifacts

When teams do try cooperative design, a common problem is to get mired in design paralysis. By this I mean meetings that seem to go round and round. It's hard for anyone to identify and discuss alternatives clearly. Discussions can easily turn into arguments where broad disagreements occur about what is important or valuable. Features of the product are seen as both required or ridiculous. The process becomes opinionated, and then little belief exists that any firm decision-making is taking place.

One of the best ways out of this situation is to get some tools or what I call *design artifacts*, which capture key information and decision-making during the product process. We already discussed a few of these artifacts, such as Personas, Scenarios, and prioritized feature lists, in previous chapters. These are the beginning of capturing information that must be agreed to by the entire team because they're the basis of making the difficult design decisions.

I would be the last person to ask for more process to be added to any company. I'm certainly not implying that reams of new reports should be written, but a large gap exists between a long report no one will read and a quick hallway meeting that's forgotten next month. These artifacts are tools that are meant to capture information and decision-making. Getting this on paper is crucial because it does two important things: 1) It forces the decisions to be made, and 2) It makes these decisions capable of being remembered.

To solve this problem, I'll discuss two additional Insights: one you do at the start of the product process and one near the end. The *Design Manifesto* is a short and simple document that, if completed, will save you untold suffering later in the project. The *SWAT Team* is a management technique for the production side of the process, to make sure the product stays on track.

INSIGHT 9 – THE DESIGN MANIFESTO

The Patient Always Stops Bleeding

A story is told of how medics in the Vietnam war were ordered to prioritize certain medical issues when on the battlefield. The most important was to stop any bleeding as quickly as possible. In a morbid twist of humor that can only come from war, the medics' reply to this edict was simple: "Hey, the patient *always* stops bleeding."

Sometimes I feel a similar attitude exists within product companies; they know they need a product plan, but whether or not it's a good plan, the guarantee is that something will eventually happen. Hey, the company *always* has a plan. The real question is will this plan kill you or save you?

It's easy to have a plan to "go north," but when you reach your first wall, if half of your team starts digging and the other half starts climbing, you don't have a good plan. The trick is not to go north, but to know *how* to go north.

While most company's *think* they have a process, they ignore or are naïve about too many deep issues to ever produce a product with Simplicity. What makes this all the more frustrating is companies are trying to create great product designs and, yet they don't change their process enough to reinforce this throughout the product cycle. Simplicity doesn't happen by itself. Simplicity can die a thousand deaths before your product ships.

Getting Started

While you'd like to believe most products start off with a blank slate and you're allowed to build nearly anything, the business reality is usually far from this ideal. Most of the time, you're given the hardware specification, when the product must ship, and how many people you will have to build it. The job is to "make something innovative" within these constraints. It's not always so overly prescribed, but the hard, realistic voice of business grinds it into you that you can't spend millions to create a product that will only bring in thousands.

The purpose of the Design Manifesto is to put together the basic goals and constraints of the project. This manifesto should only be two or three pages. It should give anyone a good idea why this project is being done, what are the "big rocks in the stream" that will make this a difficult project, and what initial decisions are required. This is a fairly standard product-management type of document. The most important difference is this document must be written jointly by the product team. Everyone from marketing, development, and design, as well as other groups, which might vary depending on your product, such as integration, testing, documentation, and so forth should be included.

Now, by the "entire team," I don't mean a complete democracy where everyone on a 200-head team has a vote. A republican model where each team has a trusted representative is much more practical. As most departments tend to have a manager or a team leader, selecting this person is usually fairly straightforward.

For companies that don't have a cultural commitment to design however, getting agreement might not be as straightforward. Getting these things written down is hard enough, but then getting agreement by the team is usually more than the company can handle. This shouldn't be a surprise. Getting all groups to agree is difficult, even in the best-run companies.

The difference is, in committed companies, they take the disagreements for what they are precursors to problems. If the teams can't agree, then the product itself will reflect this. This shows itself in poor integration, bugs, poor performance, and so forth. Of course, every project has these problems because you can't entirely eliminate them. But, if you can't even get the team to agree on the product overview, you're guaranteed to have more problems than normal.

The Design Manifesto is a tool — a simple technique to find the key issues of a project, and make sure everyone agrees to them. The following is nothing more than a list of questions that need to be written down and agreed to in the format of a template.

Design Manifesto Template
Introductory Information

Project Name

Initial Date

Product Goal

Technology Issues

Standards on which this project is based

Hardware requirements

Most challenging technical issue for this project

Key technologies with which this project interacts

Key aspects of the architecture that are inflexible

Key aspects of the architecture that can change

Key assumptions made by the architecture, such as a single user, fast response time, and memory size

Architecture, technology, and infrastructure changes considered, but which won't be done (Don't forget this one!)

Planning Issues

Date work must be done

Date programmers need to start coding

Number of programmers on the project

Graphics work required

Time scheduled for user testing/code changes

Design Issues

User Personas

Key Scenarios

Prioritized feature list

Product concept sketch

Features that will be deferred to a future release

Features that will be dropped

Several items in the list use the word "key" as in key assumptions. These are hard because they aren't a simple list, but a distillation that requires discussion and agreement. I strongly urge when putting this report together to force answers to all these questions. What amazes me is that projects will start off *without* knowing the answers to these questions. Even worse, answers exist, but they're different for each team. These situations tend to be the primary cause of integration problems and bugs much later in the project. Solving these problems in a one day offsite is *much* easier than solving them months later in late beta testing.

The Design Issues section is where to spend the most time. This is where to save time and money. By working through the user blindness tools, determine early what you'll plan to ignore. In the case of the MP3 player, we were able to ignore many tasks, such as playlists and equalization editing. What probably will happen is that working through the design issues will also force discussion/insight into many of the technical issues. This is why discussion must be early and by the entire team. Critical aspects of the product can be easily fixed if these areas are discussed early enough.

How to Do It

This Insight is the easiest of them all to explain – just fill in the previous form. Of course, the catch is broad agreement must exist.

The value of this document is the decisions it forces. And the process, I'm afraid, isn't easy.

What's more, this Design Manifesto should be short. The longest I've every seen has been three pages. It might have an appendix of the Personas and the Scenarios, and the feature lists, but it's an executive overview document and must provide a strong background of a project quickly. I've seen 30-page long marketing-positioning documents. Few people read them, which makes them a ineffective communications tool.

I recommend that various groups take responsibility for pieces of this Design Manifesto and propose solutions. In one company where I worked, my team, the design department, was responsible for filling in the whole document, talking to marketing and development to get the information, and putting it all together. The rough draft was sent out a few days before a team offsite, where we all then ran through the document and didn't leave until we came to a common agreement.

I've been in meetings where this Design Manifesto was so easy, that concern was expressed as to why we even did it. This only meant the team already had deep and shared understanding of the project and – no surprise – they didn't have any trouble shipping a good product.

I don't want to try to fool you, though. Getting agreement on the Design Manifesto won't always be easy. But I can guarantee if you can't get agreement, you're not going to ship a good product because the disagreements you see in meetings will play out all along the development cycle.

What Goes Wrong

The biggest problem that occurs is that disagreements are avoided. Everyone wants to get through this document quickly and, when differences of opinion exist, people won't speak up.

Don't let disagreements slide. Force decisions when only words are at stake. Once you start building, having a disagreement is much more expensive. The Design Manifesto is about getting key issues agreed to and shared as much as possible by the entire product team. Getting it written isn't easy. The Design Manifesto will cause arguments and it will seem like too much trouble. But it's many times easier than discovering these problems late in the product cycle.

INSIGHT 10 – THE SWAT TEAM

What It Is

While the Design Manifesto is about getting a project started properly, a SWAT Team is about finishing it properly. As a project nears completion, a hailstorm of integration problems, bug reports, and time-to-market concerns occur. If you don't keep the teamwork going, naïve decisions are made that can severely compromise the product.

Recruit a SWAT Team

The concept is fairly simple. Get a small, cross-department team, much like the one that created the Design Manifesto, and have the team review the active issues on the product. This team should include at least management, marketing, development, and interaction design. This is the internal team that reviews the current issues facing the project. What helps most is that each person is respected by the rest of their team. If you get that person to sign off on an issue, the others will most likely agree.

The team needn't be large. I would recommend three to five people, who have to meet regularly and work together. By having this cross-department core team, you create a pool of expertise with the ability to make decisions quickly and that will stick. When a decision is made, everyone has a say and all issues must be discussed. This avoids "oops" mistakes down the line.

The team meets as often as it takes. Normally, as development starts, the team might only need to meet weekly. Near the end of the project, you'll probably start meeting daily. On one project, we met every day at lunch for two hours for the last four weeks of the beta build to get through an enormous bug log.

Make Decisions

Normally, the questions asked would be about bug reports. In solving bugs, however, the programmers often raise greater concerns and large changes to the design of the product are suggested. This team must understand their primary job is to make decisions about these bugs. Using the various tools discussed, they have many ways to communicate shared, stable information, which will enable them to make decisions that aren't a matter of shouting volume but are, instead, researched information.

The purpose of the Design Manifesto is to write down the big decisions in a central place, so everyone can understand the issues and is motivated toward a common goal. Use the SWAT Team to tackle the many little problems that arise aggressively and keep the common goal intact. It shouldn't be a surprise that not everyone will buy into the common goal and honorable mistakes will be made along the way. Programmers will suggest dropping a button or changing a menu item. These are usually reasonable requests when seen only from that small corner of the project. When they're seen from the broader view, though, they would have an effect on the project.

Most companies have a similar concept, usually in the form of a bug review board or a change control team. The SWAT team is similar, except it has a broader team. I've seen a SWAT team integrated two different ways. The first is to make the bug team broader to include the SWAT functions. The other is to keep the two groups separate, letting the bug board handle the many smaller technical issues and only raise the design problems to the SWAT team. Merging the two together is the easier of the two methods and works best for smaller projects. For larger projects, it might only be practical to keep them separate because the number of bugs could easily swamp the SWAT team.

Example: Editing Contacts

When working on a digital assistant product, many applications were going into the product: a phone, a calendar, a message center, and an address book, among others. We had worked hard to give the original design a common sense of place, and we structured the applications to have a similar layout and behavior. This added significantly to the ease of learning for the product.

Once the high-level design was completed, it was handed off to a team in another country to complete the development. I warned the team about the common pressures and urged them to initiate a SWAT team to keep the design on track. Unfortunately, the team wasn't able to do that and little changes started creeping into each view. Each change wasn't so big, but the cumulative effect was significant. By the time the product had reached beta, two of the applications – those with the strongest-willed programmers – had a design altered so much that the carefully crafted uniform design was effectively gone. Given how late it was in the project, fixing the damage was impossible. The product had to ship with these grossly different application designs.

Things That Go Wrong

The SWAT team can easily get overwhelmed with bugs/issues. Most companies have a bug database of some kind and it's best to use this to track the problems.

The biggest problem faced by the SWAT team is not having enough information. A bug will come in to say that feature X must be changed to use a widget instead of a gizmo, without any details or supporting information. Send the request back to the author. The team has too much on its plate to play librarian. Make the requestor get the information before approving a change.

The next largest problem is avoiding the word "impossible." Many problems will be proposed as impossible and, therefore, need to be dropped. This is often the case, but at times, a few members of the SWAT team need to work with the problem, just as in the Embrace the Impossible Insight, to make sure an excellent, simple solution isn't available.

Disagreement within the SWAT team is to be expected. What is critical here is that one member must be the primary decision maker and that person has the final say. More often than not, I've had to sit on my hands as the project manager yanked an excellent feature because it would blow the release date. I nearly screamed every time but, in hindsight, I realized it was a mature decision because not shipping on time was the greater of two evils.

CONCLUSION

The purpose of this chapter is not to reinvent a company's design process. That isn't practical because no one process can work for everyone. The goal is to point out how implementation blindness prevents companies from executing Simplicity.

The first Insight, Design Manifesto, is a simple tool to get agreement early – at the front of a project – to try to uncover and fix the assumptions that usually kill a project. The SWAT Team Insight is nothing more than a small variation of a change review board, which is more cross-functional and tries to make informed decisions to keep the project on track.

12 Conclusion

Leadership should be born out of the understanding of the needs of those who would be affected by it.

—Marian Anderson

WHY WE'RE HERE

Shipping a well-designed product is extremely hard. This isn't only about overcoming technology and production problems, but also about coordinating a creative, stubborn, motivated, opinionated, and determined group of people to work with, not against, each other. Good design doesn't simply happen by itself. It is an active process against the thousands of problems that can derail a product. If you don't know what you want, complexity is what you'll get as a default.

High-tech companies have historically spent their energy on developing and shipping technology innovations. As products start to move out of Moore's adoption curve, it's becoming clear to most that products must be more than just technologically competent. Trying to add a "good user interface" on to a product gets the problem backward. A good user interface is composed of multiple layers, the presentation, task, and infrastructure layers, that must be explored, researched, and discussed early in the product process. Simplicity is a much stronger concept than a good user interface and it provides the focus high-tech companies need to design and implement breakthrough products. The most promising aspect of Simplicity is it's a goal that transcends the typical disciplines within most companies. Instead of something that's only taken care of by the design department, Simplicity encompasses management, marketing, project managers, designers, developers, testers, and documentation writers.

The Simplicity Shift is about the shift a company's management must take to manage the design process strategically. Companies must realize if they want to create breakthrough products, products must be set up to succeed. Strategic homework must be done to understand the target users, their tasks, and the impact of the technology on these tasks. With this homework in place, the company must then have the courage to make difficult decisions, eliminating extraneous features that add little value, and only consume development time and confuse end users. When these simplified designs uncover seemingly impossible development problems, this is a glaring indication of where innovation is hiding. Getting the team together to solve these problems is a surefire means of creating a breakthrough design.

THE PROBLEM: NAÏVE ATTITUDES

Most companies have blind spots that prevent them from creating and shipping innovative, simple designs: user blindness, feature blindness, innovation blindness, and implementation blindness. These are simply bad habits – naïve attitudes that prevent the broader product and company management from understanding what creates complexity in product design and what they can do to fix the problem. Curing each blindness isn't the responsibility of the design group. This must be a companywide goal. Creating Simplicity starts at the strategic beginning and goes all the way to the bitter, bug-fixing end.

USER BLINDNESS

User blindness comes from not understanding who the target users are and how they will end up using the product in a realistic way. Personas are a step stool to lift a shared concept of who the target user is. The most important information to know about Personas is they should be simple and understood by the entire team. The tools in this book are basic and meant to capture a rough approximation of who the target user could be. Once a company understands and uses this basic concept, it can then expand up to more sophisticated tools, such as ethnographic or field studies, to create a more robust understanding of who the target user is.

Scenarios are a simple tool to walk through the product use with a Persona. By doing this, even on a simple level, you can discover many problems that weren't previous considered.

These Insights focus a product team on the user and their tasks. They create a real user target that can be helpful in team discussions. They create design artifacts that can be shared and understood by the team. These artifacts help clarify the product goals and encourage individuals to make informed decisions. In general, these Insights give you a solid foundation to stand on, so you can make some hard Simplicity-inducing decisions.

FEATURE BLINDNESS

Feature blindness comes from confusing the need for a feature with the use of it. Too often, companies are terrorized by the feature list because it represents what must go into the product. While marketing realities are harsh, the design can't only be motivated by this list because it creates jumbled and confusing designs. I use three Insights to cure this blindness: unFeatures, The Priority Trick, and Make the Easy, Easy and the Hard, Hard.

UnFeatures is simply an extension of Scenarios, making sure the product can handle some of the basic problems that plague all consumer electronics: setup, reliability and error conditions, task flow, and a sense of place. More problems can certainly be considered, but these are the big four. By running Scenarios through these types of problems, you can find a new type of feature that should be included in the product. These additional features are often much more important than the marketing-driven list and they provide strong potential for creating a design that will meet more users needs.

The Priority Trick is the Insight you need to tame this ever-expanding list of features. By winnowing it down to a prioritized list, where you have a small set of core features listed, you get a critical understanding of what the product must do extremely well. If you push hard, you can usually also remove a few things from the list. The remaining features, while important, become secondary to the design, and will be put in after the core is designed.

Make the Easy, Easy and the Hard, Hard is how you then create this design. The core features, if they really are simplified, will free you from the mad, unending feature list that makes design so hard. By having a much smaller list, the basic design is significantly easier to see. When you have this, you can then layer on the more advanced features, but in a way that doesn't compromise the core design. This probably will make the advanced features slightly harder to access but, because they are advanced features, this isn't a significant problem. The advanced users will understand how to find them, and the new users will have a chance to understand and grow into the product. This provides a product with depth that avoids the dreaded parsing shock that typifies most complex designs today.

INNOVATION BLINDNESS

Innovation blindness comes from bad habits that inhibit innovative thinking. Innovation can't be guaranteed, but it certainly won't ever happen in a company that doesn't work hard to overcome these habits. The three Insights used here are See the Water, Embrace the Impossible, and Fail Fast.

See the Water is an attitude about actively looking for default thinking – the assumed solutions currently in use that are grafted too easily on new design situations. The two most common sources of these default solutions are digital watches and the desktop PC. While it's sometimes valuable to use these paradigms as a source of design solutions, they should always be questioned. The common problem is they're used too easily, copying interaction styles that aren't always appropriate to the task at hand.

Embrace the Impossible is about an approach to transition from the simple design and the complexities of development. Simple designs, if well motivated, aren't wrong, they simply aren't yet possible. Innovation occurs in finding a path through the technical minefield to create a solution that captures the essence of the simple design. Sometimes, the technology needs to bend slightly and, sometimes, the design must. If both sides are actively and jointly working on a solution together, instead of defending their turf, an innovative solution is usually possible.

Fail Fast understands you don't get innovation on the first try. You have to start with something, anything, because this forces you to visualize your current design. This creates understanding in a way that encourages self-criticism. The faster you create visions of your product and test these visions, the faster you will increase your understanding of the product and uncover problems in your current design. Fail Fast is the key approach to innovation because it enables you to evolve the product without having to ship a product. This not only improves the product design, but also saves enormous amounts of development time because dead-end corners of a product with little value to the customer aren't implemented.

IMPLEMENTATION BLINDNESS

Implementation blindness comes from inexperience in managing the challenges of getting a simple design to market. Companies that cure the previous three blindnesses can still never get the product to market because they don't watch the little problems that crop up and nibble away at the development. What ends up being shipped can be much less than the original design. The two Insights that best help this are the Design Manifesto and the SWAT Team.

Many products fail because a product is set up to fail. Too many issues aren't well understood or there are conflicts in the product requirements that aren't resolved until well after the product is in development. The Design Manifesto is a simple tool to collect much of the work done in the previous Insights and put them into a simple, short document that can be shared and agreed to by the product team. This simple exercise usually exposes deep misunderstandings or attitudes between the product teams, which must be resolved for an innovative product to make it out the door.

The SWAT Team is a slight variation on a Bug Review Board, common in most companies. The primary purpose of the SWAT Team is to make sure decisions made late in the product development are consistent with the original design. When problems occur at this late stage, it's far too easy to make an honorable, but naïve, decision that adversely affects the product. A SWAT Team can help eliminate some of these problems.

THE SOLUTION: ACTIVE INVOLVEMENT

The Simplicity Shift is the political change in a company needed to make sure good product design happens in a thoughtful and effective manner. Many companies have been through management improvement programs, yet few take hold. While these programs are always introduced with great enthusiasm, the management structures aren't in place to support the new program. The Simplicity Shift is nothing more than a series of tools to make the pursuit, discovery, and delivery of Simplicity a realistic and engrained part of a company culture.

Some companies feel they can't afford a strong product-design culture. Other, larger companies assume all the product design must only be the responsibility of the design department. Both of these approaches will meet with failure. This book shows how a strong product-design culture is neither complicated nor expensive to start. It also shows that good design cuts through an entire company and can't be left to a single department.

That is why the tools in this book are intentionally simple. They mean to make Simplicity a straightforward and inexpensive program to be easily integrated into a company's procedures. The cross-department use of these tools is the important first step. Once you have these communication steps in place, they can grow to incorporate deeper tools. And these tools can expand and refine the deeper understanding of your target users, who will only fuel more insightful and innovative product concepts.

Appendix: Recommended Reading

GENERALLY INTERESTING BOOKS:

The Design of Everyday Things
by Donald A. Norman (Currency/Doubleday, 1990)
Great introduction to the concept of design in everyday products. This book makes an excellent case about the importance of design or, more importantly, the lack thereof.

The Invisible Computer: Why Good Products Can Fail, the Personal Computer Is So Complex, and Information Appliances Are the Solution
by Donald A. Norman (MIT Press, 1999)
Discusses breaking out of the "PC mindset" that seems to pervade the technical industry.

The Inmates Are Running the Asylum, Why High Tech Products Drive Us Crazy, and How to Restore the Sanity
by Alan Cooper (Sams, 1999)
A bit too harsh on programmers, but a good discussion of how the technology-biased mentality can get a company into trouble.

The Trouble with Computers
by Thomas K. Landauer (MIT Press, 1996)
A slightly older book, but still an enjoyable kick in the pants. It puts the computer and its "improvements" into a much-needed perspective to help you look at the industry with a more sensitive eye.

The Visual Display of Quantitative Information
by Edward R. Tufte (Graphics Press, 2001)

This isn't a book about interactive design or usability. This book is about displaying numerical information. This might sound dull, but the book is done so well and done with such class, it's an inspiration. While the reason this book should improve interaction design isn't obvious, most designers I know thoroughly enjoy reading it.

NUTS-AND-BOLTS READING:

Handbook of Usability Testing: How to Plan, Design, and Conduct Effective Tests
by Jeffrey Rubin (John Wiley & Sons, 1994)

Contextual Design: Defining Customer-Centered Systems
by Hugh Beyer and Karen Holtzblatt (Morgan Kaufmann, 1997)

User and Task Analysis for Interface Design
by Joann T. Hackos and Janice C. Redish (John Wiley & Sons, 1998)

The Focus Group: A Strategic Guide to Organizing, Conducting, and Analyzing the Focus Group Interview
by Jane Farley Templeton (McGraw-Hill, 1996)

Index

A

analog timers, on microwave ovens, 58, 60–61
Anderson, Marian, 161
Apple computers, 30
  early users of, 24–25
  hierarchical menus on, 31
  Newton (handheld computer) by, 117, 118
  Personal File Sharing on, 87–88
  print options example from, 84–85
AutoCook button, on microwave ovens, 61–62,
  68–69, 71, 72

B

base stations, for MP3 players, 99
battery power, for MP3 players, 99
Bluetooth, 18–20, 32–33, 75, 122–23
Boorstin, Daniel, 23
bugs, 158, 159

C

cars
  common design for, 115
  playing MP3 players in, 97
  starting, 29
cell phones, *see* mobile telephones
Churchill, Sir Winston, 57
clocks
  digital watches, 115, 116
  on heater timer, 143–45, 147
  see also timers
complexity, 11
  tied to flexibility, 12–13
computers
  turning off, 29–30
  see also Apple computers; personal
    computers
consumers, innovation life cycles for,
  24–27
Cooper, Alan, 2

cordless telephones, 25–26
corporate culture, 39–40
costs
  of controls for microwave ovens, 71
  of heater timer design, 144
  of MP3 players, 111
  of User Centered Design, 3–4
Crosby, Philip, 4–5, 21

D

design
  commonalties and standards in, 115
  "Failing Fast" in, 124
  of heater timer, 135
  simplicity in, 5–6
  sketching in, 125–29
  target users for, 41–42
  user testing of, 130–31
design artifacts, 151–52
designers
  conflicts between programmers and, 119
  idealism of, 123
  implementation blindness of, 149
  programmers working closely with, 121
Design Manifestos, 152–58, 166
desktop interfaces, 115, 116
digital timers
  on heater timer, 144–45
  on microwave ovens, 58, 60–61
digital watches, 115, 116
Director (program), 129
displays
  fonts for, 85–86
  on heater timer, 135
  on MP3 players, 93–94, 98–99, 104–6

E

early adopters, 24–27
easy/hard tradeoffs, 17

e-mail, 28–29
  deleting, 77–78
  horizontal layout for, 126
  on mobile telephones, 116, 119–21
errors
  complex dialog boxes for, 87–88
  recovery from, 76–77
ethnographic studies, 42
expert users, 16

F

"Failing Fast," 124, 165
feature blindness, 7, 73, 163–64
feature lists, 73–74, 89–90
features
  flexibility in use of, 83–85
  layering, 85–86
  prioritizing, 20, 80–82, 164
  Simplicity in mix of, 12
  unFeatures and, 75–76, 79–80
  user personas and, 44–45
featuritis, 62
field studies, 45–47
Flash (program), 129
flexibility, 12–13
FM transmitter, for MP3 players, 97, 102
focus groups, 45
folders, for e-mail, 116, 120
fonts, for displays, 85–86
functionality, 12

G

GPRS telephones, 35–39
  error recovery on, 77
  scenarios on use of, 52, 53

H

hardware, for MP3 players, 93, 102
headsets
  for mobile telephones, 18–20, 122
  for MP3 players, 96
heater timer, 133–34
  core design of, 140–43
  design of, 135
  personas for, 137–38
  programming, 135–37
  scenarios for, 138–40
  simplified design of, 144–48
Heinlein, Robert, 113

I

implementation
  Design Manifestos in, 152–57, 166
  SWAT teams for, 157–60

implementation blindness, 7, 149–50,
    165–66
infrastructure layer (of user interface), 28–29
innovation blindness, 7, 113–14, 164–65
innovation life cycles, 24–27
innovators, 24
interactive demos, 129–30
interfaces, *see* user interfaces
Internet, music on, 99

K

Kay, Alan, 73

L

layering features, 85–86
life cycles in technology adoption, 24–27

M

Macintosh computers, *see* Apple computers
"magic," 121
marketing
  additional features added to microwave ovens
    because of, 62
  target users for, 41–42
messaging application for mobile telephones,
    13–14, 28–29
microwave ovens, 57–60
  AutoCook buttons on, 68–69
  costs of controls on, 71
  design of controls for, 72
  features on, 61–62
  flexibility in use of, 83–84
  functionality of controls for, 69–71
  persona and scenarios used on problem of, 62–64
  power-level controls on, 66–68
  timers on, 60–61, 64–66
mobile telephones
  bad design in messaging application for,
    13–14
  Bluetooth for, 18–20, 32–33, 122–23
  e-mail on, 116, 119–21
  GPRS, 35–39
  locking keypads on, 31–32
  Nokia's designs for, 14–17
  text messaging on, 28–29
Moore, Geoffrey A., 23–26, 33, 57
MP3 players, 91–95, 111–12
  costs of, 111
  design of, 102–3
  personas for, 95–96
  playing music on, 103–6
  recording music on, 106–9
  scenarios for, 97–102
  settings for, 110–11

N

navigational models, 78–79
Newton (handheld computer), 117, 118
Nielson, Jacob, 130
Nokia (firm), 14–17
Norman, Donald A., 2

O

Orwell, George, 27

P

Palm PDAs, 117
paper prototypes, 130
parsing shock, 13
personal computers (PCs)
  moving e-mail to mobile telephones from, 119–21
  using MP3 players with, 99, 102, 103, 110–11
personal digital assistants (PDAs)
  display fonts on, 85–86
  Newton, 117, 118
personas (of target users), 43–50, 162–63
  in heater timer example, 137–40
  in microwave oven problem, 62–64, 72
  in MP3 player example, 95–102
  prioritizing features for, 81–82
  using scenarios with, 54–55
playlists, 99, 105
power-level controls, 66–68
PowerPoint (program), 129
presentation layer (of user interface), 27–28
prioritizing features, 80–82, 90, 164
  layering of, 85–86
products
  feature lists for, 73–74
  scenarios of use of, 50–54
  setting up, 76
product teams
  Design Manifestos used by, 153, 156
  innovation blindness in, 113
  innovation discouraged in, 117–18
  layering of features understood by, 89
  programmers and designers working together on, 121
  SWAT teams and, 157–60
  user personas for, 48
  working together on, 150
programmers, 20
  conflicts between designers and, 119
  deep architectural solutions sought by, 123
  designers working closely with, 121
programming, of heater timer, 135–37

Q

quality, 4–5, 21
queuing, 94

R

recording, on MP3 players, 100–101, 107–9
repetitive tasks, 77–78
Russell, Bertrand, 1

S

Sampter, Jessie, 11
saving data, on Quartz PDA, 117
scaffolding of functions, 16
scenarios, 50–54, 121, 163
  in microwave oven problem, 63–64, 72
  in MP3 player example, 96–102
  using personas with, 54–55
screens, see displays
scroll bars, 93–94, 115
scroll wheels, 99, 111
settings for MP3 players, 110–11
setup for products
  for heater timer, 135–39
  for MP3 player, 96, 110–11
  for new products, 76
sketching, in design, 125–29
soft buttons, 93
spreadsheets, 118
start/stop buttons, 65
Stevenson, Adlai, 91
surprise packages, 25–26
SWAT teams, 157–60, 166

T

target users, 41–43, 162
  personas of, 43–50
  scenarios of product use by, 50–54
task layer (of user interface), 28
technology adoption life cycles, 24–27
telephones
  cordless, 25–26
  GPRS, 35–39
  mobile, 13–20
  tents, 24
text messaging, 13–14, 28–29
timers
  heater timer, 133–48
  on microwave ovens, 58, 60–61, 64–66
Tufte, Edward, 13

U

unFeatures, 75–76, 79–80, 89–90, 163–64
usability testing, 130–31

user blindness, 6, 162–63
User Centered Design (UCD), 2
   costs of, 3–4
user interfaces, 161
   fiction of, 23
   layers of, 27–31
   Simplicity in, 12, 13
users
   expert users, 16
   personas of, 43–50
   reporting errors to, 77
   research to analyze, 42–43
   scenarios of product use by, 50–54

target users, 41–42
user testing, 130–31

V

van Gogh, Vincent, 41
VCRs, 76
volume control, on MP3 players, 96, 102

W

Wirth, Nicholas, 133
World Wide Web, 35–39

Printed in the United States
by Bookmasters

Printed in the United States
By Bookmasters